EMPOWHER

REAL STORIES • BOLD VOICES
GLOBAL IMPACT

EMPOWHER

**REAL STORIES • BOLD VOICES
GLOBAL IMPACT**

BOOK 1

A Collaboration of Global Leaders

LEADING LADIES

Putting Words
Melbourne Australia

A catalogue record for this book is available from the National Library of Australia.

ISBN: 978-1-7637042-5-1 (Paperback)
978-1-7637042-9-9 (E-book)

Produced by Putting Words
Putting Words
PO Box 5062

Wonga Park, Victoria, 3115
Australia.
www.puttingwords.com

Dedication

To every woman who has carried a dream quietly,
and kept going when no one saw her effort.
To the daughters who dare to rise,
and the mothers who taught us how.
To the voices that shake ceilings,
and the hearts that heal the world.
May we lift each other higher,
and continue to empower.

Thank you to every woman who stepped forward in these pages, who spoke from the heart, and chose courage to make a difference.

She rises, not for glory,
but to open doors unseen.
She carries light for others,
and grows hope where she has been.
Together we stand stronger,
with courage as our guide.
For when one woman EMPOWERs,
she helps all women rise.

Contents

Introduction

There are moments in our lives that change us forever. Not because everything suddenly becomes easy, but because we finally decide to rise, to speak, to lead, and to believe that our voice matters. This book was born from one of those moments. A moment shared between women across the world who know what it means to fall down, get back up, and stand stronger than before. It comes from a collective desire to use our stories not as weight that drags us backwards, but as power that propels us forward.

This compilation book is not written by people who had everything handed to them. It's written by women who fought invisible battles, who stood in boardrooms where their presence was questioned, who led families through uncertainty, who built businesses from nothing, who worked tirelessly behind the scenes without applause, who carried the emotional weight of those they love, and who still found the courage to create something better. Every chapter, every story, every woman in these pages has earned her voice, her wisdom, and her leadership through experience. And she shares it not to impress you, but to empower you.

Because empowered women don't just break barriers — they build bridges.

In my life as a conscious leader, international trainer, and professional speaker, I have met thousands of women in every corner of this beautiful world. I've sat with women in corporate offices in London, listened to mothers in Uganda who are raising orphaned children with unwavering hope, laughed with entrepreneurs in New York, shared tea with leaders in Dubai and China, and hugged women in tiny classrooms in rural villages in India and business schools in Saudi. No matter where we stood on the planet, we shared the same human truth: **Women are powerful when we choose to stand together.**

The Ripple Effect of Empowerment

Empowerment is not a moment. It's a ripple.

It begins quietly — sometimes as a whisper, sometimes as a plea, sometimes as a decision to take just one step forward. And then, like water, it spreads. One woman learns something new, gains confidence, finds her voice, launches a dream, makes a choice that changes her entire life. She uses her voice and her actions to uplift another woman. Then that woman lifts someone else, and the ripple continues.

The ripple of empowerment crosses countries, communities, languages, cultures, and circumstances. It creates opportunities for those who have never been given one. It builds leaders where others once only saw followers. It elevates voices that were silenced or dismissed. And it proves something incredibly important:

When women are empowered, the world becomes smarter, safer, stronger, and more compassionate.

Our stories matter not only because they tell us where we come from, but because they shape where we can go. They become beacons of possibility. They remind others that leadership does not come from perfection. Leadership comes from resilience, self-awareness, action, empathy, and courage. And it is these qualities that echo throughout this book.

Why We Lead

There is a persistent myth that leadership is a title, an office, a level of authority, or a position earned at the top. But women have always known something deeper: Leadership is who we are when no one is watching. It's how we communicate when emotions run high. It's how we serve when there is no promise of applause. It's how we love when we are hurting. It's how we continue to show up — even when we don't feel ready.

Women lead in their kitchens and in their communities. They lead in parliaments, in schools, on farms, in science labs, in hospitals, in startups, in banking halls, in humanitarian missions, and in homes. Leadership is not limited by where we are — it is defined by how we think, how we behave, and the difference we choose to make.

We lead because we care. Because we must. Because there is always someone watching, learning, hoping, or needing someone to walk first. We lead because if we don't, someone who lacks empathy might.

We lead because our stories show others what is possible.

And this compilation, this movement, this legacy of Leading Ladies, is proof that no woman ever needs to rise alone. Together, we elevate humanity.

The Power of Story in Leadership

For years, I have studied human behaviour, body language, communication, and leadership. I've seen first-hand how what we think, feel, and believe shapes our external actions. I've studied leaders who influence teams, shift cultures, and spark movements. And one truth continues to reveal itself: **The most influential leaders are storytellers.**

A story holds the power to shift a mindset faster than a lecture. It opens hearts before it changes minds. It disarms fear by saying, "I've been there too." It bridges differences by reminding us that humanity is shared. When a woman shares her truth, she doesn't just liberate herself — she gives others permission to step into theirs.

This is why this compilation of stories matter. It is a testament to the collective voice of women who are willing to share their journey so others can find courage in their own. You will read stories that heal, stories that disrupt, stories that challenge, and stories that inspire action. You may see yourself in these pages. You may find tears where you did not expect them. You may feel anger, strength, laughter, relief, clarity, or sudden bravery. You may rethink what is possible for you.

That is the power of story.

A Tapestry of Voices, Cultures, and Calls to Action

Each woman in this compilation comes from different experiences, different industries, different families, different cultures. Some have built businesses. Some have raised nations from their kitchen tables. Some have reinvented themselves after heartbreak. Some have led communities without ever being given a leadership title. Some have triumphed after trauma. Some have mastered their craft against all odds. Some are still finding their way — and that is leadership too.

Together, we create a global tapestry. A tapestry woven not with threads of perfection, but with threads of truth, vulnerability, strategy, humour, impact, grit, grace, and determination. These stories invite you to listen, to learn, to feel, and to step forward differently. Not by copying anyone else's path, but by claiming your own.

There is brilliance in diversity. There is beauty in collaboration. And there is unstoppable force in unified intention. This book is a shared intention to ignite more women leaders everywhere. Not someday. Not after permission. Not after we feel ready. But now.

The Conscious Leader Within

Throughout my career, I've taught leaders how to communicate with clarity, connect with trust, and lead with intention. And I've seen how quickly external success collapses when internal awareness is neglected. Conscious leadership isn't a technique — it's a way of being. It asks us to understand our emotions, respect our values, and align our behaviours with a purpose greater than ourselves. It demands presence. It demands honesty. It demands empathy and accountability.

Women are uniquely positioned to lead consciously. From a young age, many of us are taught to read people, anticipate needs, nurture solutions, negotiate peace, and think of others before ourselves. These skills — once dismissed as "soft" — are now recognised as competitive advantages in the future of leadership. Emotional intelligence, ethical decision-making, relational influence, and inclusive communication are no longer "nice qualities." They are business imperatives. They are the tools of global change. And women have mastered them for generations.

Still, conscious leadership requires one crucial shift: We must stop apologising for being capable. We must stop shrinking so that others feel comfortable. We must own our expertise. We must honour our worth. We must allow our presence to take up space. We must raise our voices with confidence, not arrogance; with intention, not noise.

The conscious leader is not the loudest voice in the room. She is the one who listens deeply, speaks truthfully, acts ethically, and leads with care. She makes decisions not from ego, but from awareness. She builds not just teams, but trust. She influences not from fear, but through example. And she understands that leadership is not a spotlight — it is a responsibility.

This compilation is a mirror for conscious leadership. As you read, ask yourself not just What did she do? but What does this awaken in me? Because empowerment is not passive. It is participation.

From Hardship to Heroism

Many of the women in these pages have walked through fire — yet they don't identify as victims. They are visionaries. They turn hardship into wisdom. They turn pain into purpose. They turn silence into advocacy. They turn obstacles into opportunities. They reinvent. They rebuild. They rise. And they show us that leadership is not about never falling — it is about refusing to stay down.

Our scars are not shameful; they are proof of our survival. They remind us that we have strength we never asked to develop, but strength we must now use. That is the heroism of women. Not perfection. Not invincibility. But evolution.

We grow stronger not by avoiding struggle, but by moving through it consciously. We unlock our worth not by waiting to be chosen, but by choosing ourselves. And we inspire others not by having all the answers, but by sharing the truth of how we found them.

A Call to Rise

This book is an invitation and a challenge. It asks you to see yourself as a leader — not tomorrow, not when you finally feel ready, but now. Leadership is not a destination; it's a decision. A decision to make a difference, to communicate with intention, to show kindness without being walked over, to set boundaries without guilt, to live from values instead of fears, and to take action even when it scares you.

You are reading this for a reason. Something in you is ready for more. More voice. More growth. More clarity. More self-worth. More impact. More influence. More alignment. More power — not power over people, but power within yourself.

This is your moment. Every chapter in this book is a reminder that you are not behind, you are not too late, you are not unqualified, and you are not alone. Whatever you have lived through, whatever you are building, whatever you are healing, whatever you are hoping for — there is a place for you at the table of leadership. And if there isn't one yet, you have the ability to build it.

The Global Legacy of Leading Ladies

This compilation from leading ladies is part of a larger global movement to empower and educate women everywhere. We are building a legacy where women raise women, where leadership begins with connection... not correction, and where success is shared rather than competed for. A legacy where every woman knows she is capable of influence, innovation, and impact.

The women in these pages lift not only themselves, but others. They create change not only for their own families or communities, but for future generations. They rise not only for personal success, but for global transformation. This is the legacy of Leading Ladies. A legacy of unity. A legacy of action. A legacy of embodied leadership that will outlive us all.

To the Reader

As you turn each page, allow yourself to do three things:

Feel. Learn. And act.

Let these stories land where they need to in your life. Let them challenge beliefs that no longer serve you. Let them sharpen the edges of your confidence. Let them comfort your heart, strengthen your voice, and awaken your vision.

Empowerment is not something we wait for. It is something we claim. So, claim it. Own it. Practice it. Speak it. Live it. And then, pass it on.

Because the world doesn't just need more thought leaders the world needs more thoughtful leaders.

Actually, the world needs YOU ... more women who lead. A big thank you to Dr Mary Jane Alvero, Dr LouAnne Boyd, Dr Mini Kaur Rattu, Sneha Villalva, Shivani Gupta, Ashley Levin, Jeanette Allom-Hill, Jayne Hansford, Fisayo Odunaike, Margaret Kelly, Tracy Tully, Apoorva Rastogi, Alex Harris, Josanne Falla, Jodi Gagné, Larisa Vakulina, Julie Cass, Elee Joven, Chris Childs, Aisha Rodriguez, and Cassandra Carson, without you we would not have these stories to share.

A story shared is a problem halved. Please enjoy the stories, insights, and wisdom woven through the next 22 chapters.

With deep gratitude

Catherine Molloy
Founder
Leading Ladies Lunches

The Corporate Queen
by Dr Mary Jane Alvero

"Because true queens don't just wear crowns
— they lift others to wear theirs too."

Rising Again:
Finding Strength Through Love and Understanding

There was a time when I didn't feel empowered — when my first marriage failed. My second marriage isn't perfect either, but it's much better than the first.

For me, work has never been the issue. I can work 24 hours without pressure or tension and still feel happy. But when it comes to family matters — that's where my world can collapse. I'm like that.

So how do I rise again?

I communicate. Always.

When things get heavy or painful, I express what I feel. Sometimes not verbally — but through writing. Writing helps me say everything that's inside my heart. It's how I find clarity, peace, and strength again.

And my husband supports me through that. When I open my heart to him, he listens and speaks with kindness. He has this gentle way of helping me find my faith again. Sometimes his words convince me, sometimes they don't — but I always take them to heart.

I've learned that in marriage, there will always be ups and downs. The key is acceptance — understanding that perfection isn't the goal.

I remind myself that my happiness cannot and should not be defined by anyone else's actions or shortcomings. My joy is my responsibility.

And one more thing — I've learned not to expect too much from others. Whether it's my husband or anyone else, I give what I can with an open heart, without expecting the same in return. That mindset brings peace.

Because empowerment, for me, isn't about having control over everything — it's about finding peace in my heart, faith in my path, and strength to rise again, no matter what.

Embracing Uniqueness and Complementing Strengths

I do not compare myself to other people. I know that each of us is unique in our own ways. For example, I may be very good at decision-making and strategy, while someone else excels in execution or performance. One person might be more functional, another more strategic — it doesn't make anyone better or worse.

I know my own strengths and weaknesses. I'm strong in decision-making and planning, but I don't enjoy running errands or managing every small detail. That's where my personal assistant comes in. She handles the logistics efficiently, while I focus on the bigger picture. Similarly, when organizing programs or projects, I might outline everything immediately, but my secretary brings it to life in a highly effective way. Without her, the process would be much slower.

Each of us has different talents. Artists, for example, may not be technically inclined, but their imagination and vision create things only they can fully understand. That uniqueness is powerful.

I remind myself that whatever I have is uniquely me. I don't compare myself to others, and I don't set unrealistic expectations — whether it's in leading my team, working with colleagues, or in life. Where there are gaps, I find ways to complement and support.

This mindset also applies to marriage and relationships. Marriage isn't about getting exactly what we want — it's about complementing each other. Filling in the gaps where needed, offering support where possible. Communication is the number one factor in any relationship — business, family, friendship, or marriage. Without it, it becomes difficult to grow, understand, and thrive together.

Understanding and Leading with Empathy

I'm not bragging, but one of my strengths is that I can sense how people are feeling. If I have 700 people with me, I can tell if someone is feeling low or not empowered. I make it a point to connect with my team regularly — once a week, I mingle with different departments. For example, this week it might be the HR team, next week the finance team.

We don't talk about business. We talk about life. Just life. We enjoy the day, take a break, and detach from the pressures we all face. I know my team is under a lot of stress, especially because many of them are expatriates, far from their families. Their families are a central support system in their culture, and being away can be challenging. Understanding this requires patience, empathy, and presence.

Even myself, I manage 10 businesses — the pressures are huge. That's why having a very capable personal assistant is essential for time management. She reminds me of things I might forget, allowing me to focus on my team and my responsibilities.

Cultural understanding is also key. My husband is Arab, and our cultural and religious backgrounds are different from mine. For instance, in his faith, a man can have up to four wives simultaneously. I grew up in a Roman Catholic family where divorce is not an option and my mother was the only wife of my father. Embracing these differences requires respect, awareness, and acceptance. But at the end of the day, it's still your decision whether to take the marriage or not — and that choice is always yours.

Balancing Leadership and Family Dynamics

Some men may say, "No, I will not divorce," while others may say, "If you cannot stay with my other wife, then you have a choice." For me, miscommunications with my husband or his family can be challenging. I often feel insecure about my faith and have to remind myself that the status or achievements I reach are not just for me — they are for the family.

Sometimes, men struggle when their partner is in a stronger position professionally or earns more than them. My husband once told me, "Honey, you are not the CEO in the home. I am still the leader of the family." I was shocked. I had been so used to managing people, creating strategies, and making decisions at work that, unknowingly, I had carried the same habits into my home life. I wasn't doing it deliberately, but it came out naturally. It was a wake-up call to recognize the different dynamics at home.

Even with children, the rules are different now. My daughter once told me, "Mama, you cannot enforce me to do things that are not okay for you." She attends the Australian International School, and the way children express themselves today is different from when I was growing up. Sometimes, they are right.

For instance, yesterday my daughter was upset because her father insists she comes straight home after school, rather than spending time with friends. She is very sociable and involved in community leadership activities. When she called me crying, I understood her perspective — but her father was following his rules. Moments like these remind me that empathy, listening, and understanding each individual's needs are just as important at home as they are in leadership.

Applying Leadership Skills at Home

Sometimes, being a parent or a partner requires the same strategic thinking as being a CEO — but adapted for home. Recently, I guided my daughter to evaluate her after-school activities. She listed each activity and assessed its impact on her studies — how it would help or hinder her learning, how much time it would take, and its overall value.

She began ranking her activities, assigning numbers and percentages to each. Through this process, she realized some activities weren't worth doing — they didn't provide value. This mirrors what I do in business. In the workplace, we assess risks, set priorities, and decide what to escalate and what to manage without intervention. At home, I simplify these concepts for her.

The same principle applies to my relationship with my husband. Some topics I choose to let pass, while others I escalate — addressing only what truly affects us. With my team at work, the same logic applies. Strategy is essential in leadership, whether at home, in business, or in life.

Empowerment Through Happiness, Relationships, and Knowledge

Even though I have more than 700 employees and just two children — one daughter and one son — I've learned that my mindset shapes my day. Every morning, I decide to be happy. Whatever happens, I start the day with positivity. This simple practice has a profound impact.

The second source of empowerment for me is my relationships — with my family, my team, and the people around me. Nurturing these connections strengthens me and gives me energy to lead effectively.

The third source is knowledge. Being knowledgeable makes you a better communicator. And if you can communicate well, you hold incredible influence. As I like to say, you become a queen — capable of leading, inspiring, and even ruling your own world.

That's why I've dreamed of becoming a TEDx speaker. Listening to TEDx speakers has always inspired me because their stories resonate deeply. Sharing knowledge and experiences in a way that empowers others is something I truly love.

Empowering Through Leadership and Teamwork

The people you surround yourself with define your journey. I always work with good people. My core board of directors empowers me. They don't treat me like an ordinary employee; they challenge me, set clear targets, and expect me to deliver. This dynamic energizes me — I am happy, and I consistently meet my goals.

I personally look after everyone on my team, including corporate managers. I talk to them, understand their needs, and evaluate what support they require to succeed.

For example, one manager is an Arab strategist who is exceptional at generating results but prefers to work behind the scenes and struggles with communication. Another manager is a strong communicator but isn't meeting sales targets. In these situations, I assess their strengths and gaps, figuring out how to complement their skills and help them perform at their best.

Not everyone is the same. Each person is different, and understanding their unique abilities and limitations is key to empowering them and achieving success as a team.

Evaluating and Developing Team Strengths

In situations where a team member is struggling or not fully expressing their potential, I evaluate what is lacking. Not all people are the same — everyone has different strengths and weaknesses.

For example, one manager may have the skills but lacks confidence to speak publicly, or fears making mistakes. Another may be capable of leading discussions but isn't following up effectively. In these cases, I stay closely in contact with the HR manager to track activities, training, and development programs for our corporate managers. If I notice gaps, I address them immediately — identifying needs, recommending training, and ensuring follow-through.

I can do this effectively because I started from the lower ranks myself. I rose step by step — from the working level, to functional roles, supervisory positions, managerial roles, and beyond. Having experienced every level of the organization gives me a deep understanding of people's challenges and how to support their growth. This perspective allows me to lead with empathy while maintaining performance and results.

Championing Inclusion and Fairness

The other day, I faced a situation that left me deeply disappointed. One of my directors is a UAE national, and within their cultural framework, LGBTQ+ individuals are not accepted in the workplace. From the very beginning, I was told this.

However, I cannot discriminate against someone who is qualified and performs well. When the board of directors instructed me to remove this individual, I was frustrated. I reminded them that managing the team is my responsibility, and their role is to set vision and targets, not to interfere with staffing decisions.

I explained that removing this person would violate workers' rights and constitute unlawful retaliation. Even our HR manager supported me. But cultural and religious biases made the situation challenging.

I come from a culture where LGBTQI+ individuals are accepted — my best friend is gay — and for me, inclusion is fundamental. My goal has always been gender and diversity inclusion, ensuring everyone has the opportunity to contribute based on their abilities, regardless of identity.

At work, everyone deserves equal rights and opportunities. Even individuals who have made mistakes in the past, like former criminals, deserve a chance to reintegrate and live with dignity. For me, the principle is clear: as long as someone is not harming others, they deserve respect, fairness, and the right to thrive.

Leading with Integrity

In every situation I face, I take time to evaluate — to ask, what is lacking? Because not all people are the same. They each have different strengths, personalities, and fears. Some leaders love to speak and share, while others struggle to find their voice. That's why I stay closely connected with HR — to understand our people, their activities, and their growth.

When I see something missing, I act. I've walked every step — from the working level to functional, then supervisory, and finally managerial. That journey gives me perspective. I understand what it feels like to be at the bottom, and that's why I can lead with compassion and clarity at the top.

But leadership is not always easy. In my role, I've witnessed decisions that broke my heart. One of the hardest challenges I've faced is discrimination.

I came from a culture — the Philippines — where people are accepted for who they are. For me, it's simple: as long as someone performs well and treats others with respect, they deserve the same opportunity as anyone else. Everyone deserves a chance — even those who have made mistakes in the past. Leadership means standing up for fairness, even when it costs you comfort.

There were moments when I felt powerless — like my wings were being broken. But even then, I reminded myself that integrity and compassion are my true strength.

Women Empowering Others

I believe women are empowered from the moment they are born. From childhood, responsibility is already placed in our hands — to nurture, to care, to build families, and to lead. Whether married or single, women carry strength that moves families, workplaces, and communities forward.

That's why I say it's not about women empowerment, but about women empowering others.

To empower others, you must first be a role model — in your words, your actions, your values, and even the way you dress or carry yourself. People are always watching, learning, and being influenced by your example.

For me, sharing my story has become one of the most powerful ways to empower others. I receive letters from people saying, "Madam, you inspired me with your story." That is the greatest reward — to know that by being open and authentic, I can help others rise.

I've learned that empowerment is not a speech; it's a reflection of your daily choices. The way you treat people. The way you stay strong. The way you lift others when they feel small.

Now, at 56, I know my purpose clearly — to be a role model and to empower others through example.

A Legacy Reaching the Sky

Do you know Burj Khalifa the tallest tower in the world? It was built between 2005 and 2009 — and that structure is a symbol of my success.

My company was the official laboratory for the Burj Khalifa. We tested all the materials — from the foundations underground to the steel and concrete that rise into the sky. The strength of the Burj Khalifa represents our achievement, our integrity, and our dedication.

Whenever I feel sad or discouraged, I go and look at it. I stand there and remind myself: I did something great. I helped build something that touches the sky. So why should I be sad? I don't deserve to be sad.

Every day, thousands of people visit that tower. And I know, deep in my heart, that our work helped make it strong. That's my legacy. They even featured me in an article titled "The Filipino Engineers Behind the Success of Burj Khalifa." To see our work in the Guinness World Records fills me with pride and gratitude.

The Burj Khalifa isn't just a building — it's a reminder that with integrity, empathy, and belief in yourself, you can rise above anything.

It stands as a symbol of what happens when you lead with heart, stay true to your values, and empower others along the way.

The Corporate Queen

They call me The Corporate Queen — and that name has become my brand here in the UAE.

It's not a title of vanity; it's a reflection of what people see in me — a woman who rose through hard work, integrity, and the courage to challenge perceptions.

When I first came to the UAE, many people carried the belief that Filipino women were only meant for household work. There was a stigma — a limiting view of what we could become. But through dedication, professionalism, and by leading with heart, I changed that perception.

Now, people see Filipino women not only as employees, but as **leaders, entrepreneurs, and changemakers**.

We have proven that we can lead with grace and strength, that we can transform teams, build businesses, and contribute at the highest levels of leadership.

For me, this title — The Corporate Queen — represents every Filipino woman who dared to dream beyond expectations. It stands for every woman who rose from humble beginnings, who fought bias with brilliance, and who continues to empower others by example.

Because true queens don't just wear crowns — **they lift others to wear theirs too.**

Three Empowerment Tips from Dr. Mary Jane

1. Prioritize Your Well-Being

Empowerment starts with taking care of yourself. A healthy mind and a healthy body are the foundation for everything you do. Self-care matters — how you feel inside shows on your face and in your energy. Every morning, remind yourself: I have to be happy today, no matter what happens. Positivity in the morning sets the tone for your entire day.

2. Nurture Your Relationships

The people around you are a source of strength. Your family, your team, and your community all contribute to your sense of empowerment. Strong relationships provide support, perspective, and inspiration — and they remind you that leadership is not just about what you achieve alone.

3. Grow Your Knowledge

Knowledge is power, but only when you can share it effectively. Being knowledgeable and a strong communicator allows you to inspire, lead, and influence others. When your mind, heart, and knowledge align, you can rule your world. You are the queen.

"When your mind, heart, and knowledge align, you become unstoppable. You are the queen."

About Dr. Mary Jane

Dr. Mary Jane Alvero is a pioneering and highly decorated CEO in the United Arab Emirates, widely known as "The Corporate Queen." She has redefined the image of Filipino women in the Middle East by demonstrating that strategic leadership, compassion, and resilience can thrive together. From modest beginnings, she has risen to lead a workforce of more than 700 employees, becoming a respected executive and an inspiration to women across the globe. Her leadership philosophy centers on choosing happiness, valuing relationships, and embracing knowledge as a key to empowerment.

A proud Filipino, she played a vital role in the success of Dubai's iconic Burj Khalifa through her company's function as the official materials testing laboratory—making the world's tallest tower a testament to her strength and perseverance.

Dr. Mary Jane's excellence has earned her numerous international recognitions, including the Pamana ng Pilipino Award (2012), Emirates Business Woman of the Year (2008), BLAS F. Ople Award (2009), Bagong Bayani Award (2009), Asia CEO Awards – Global Filipino Executive of the Year (2020), Emirates Woman – Woman of the Year (2013), and a feature in Forbes Woman Middle East (2014), among many others celebrating her leadership and influence.

Beyond her corporate achievements, she advocates for inclusion, guides emerging leaders, and champions women's empowerment. Her journey reminds others that authentic leadership has the power to uplift, inspire, and create lasting change.

[in]
dr-mary-jane-alvero-phd-mba-bsche-5ab13464

🌐 primegroup.ae

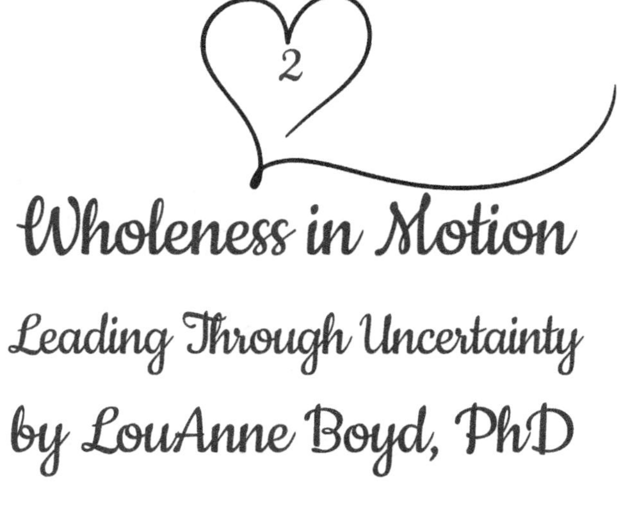

Wholeness in Motion

Leading Through Uncertainty

by LouAnne Boyd, PhD

"Wholeness isn't what happens after we're healed
— it's what carries us through the healing."

The Retreat

The wind coming off the South Pacific was brisk that March morning, salted and alive. At the Q Station cottages in Manly, the sea stretched wide and blue below the veranda railings, and the eucalyptus trees whispered in a language older than any of us. I had come here for a writing retreat with Catherine Molloy, hoping that distance and quiet might help me find a way to exhale after years of pushing toward tenure. The weight of achievement had begun to feel like armor—protective, but heavy.

As the sun began to set over Sydney Harbour, the sky melted from gold to rose, and we gathered barefoot on the deck of the old Q Station cottage, our notebooks scattered among plates of charcuterie and half-filled glasses. The air smelled of eucalyptus and sea salt, the light catching on our pens as if blessing the words we were brave enough to write. Catherine invited us to take turns reading aloud, her voice calm and steady against the distant rhythm of the waves. When it was my turn, my hands trembled as I lifted the pages—pieces of Year of the Mongoose, still raw and uncertain. I began to read, pausing halfway through, hearing myself editing as I spoke. I looked up at Catherine and confessed, "I'm changing the words as I read them." She tilted her head, eyes curious, and said gently, "Interesting," the single word both an observation and a mirror. In that moment I felt her seeing not just the words, but the woman beneath them—my inner truth surfacing, hesitant and electric in the amber light. Catherine held my gaze, steady and kind, as if to say, keep going. That night I understood writing not as product but as pulse—the body's way of translating what the heart already knows.

Held in Circle, Sea, and Sisterhood

Each day that followed carried that same hum of vulnerability and discovery. We wrote in quiet corners of the cottages, sometimes side by side, sometimes alone by the window overlooking the sea. Pens moved steadily, occasionally halting when memory demanded breath. Tears came easily; so did laughter. At night we gathered again to share meals lovingly prepared by our exquisite chef Jayne, toasting to courage and craft, to the strange relief of being fully ourselves among witnesses. Still, even in the gentleness of that circle, I could feel a tension humming beneath the quiet—the old, familiar worry that maybe I wasn't enough, that maybe all those late nights and conference papers still wouldn't add up to security.

The final morning arrived bright and clear, the kind of day that feels like a benediction. Sunlight poured through the cottage windows, catching on our scattered drafts and half-drunk mugs of tea. Catherine gathered us once more, asking each of us to read something that captured what we had discovered during the week. My heart pounded as I unfolded my pages—words I had written in that raw, shimmering space between fear and freedom.

Something shifted in me then, something I had been holding back for years. Writing had always been part of my work, but this was different—it was writing as embodiment, as truth. I felt lighter, as though I had finally given myself permission to exist outside the metrics of academia.

When my turn came, I read the final lines aloud, my voice steadier now, carried by the rhythm of the sea just beyond the windows. When I finished, the room was still—no applause, just breath and presence. Catherine met my eyes again, that same look of quiet witnessing, and nodded as if to acknowledge the crossing I had made. Something in me settled. Writing had never felt so physical, so alive; it was no longer a task to complete but a conversation with my own becoming.

Tenure and the Illusion of Arrival

That night I barely slept. Outside, the waves kept their patient rhythm while I lay awake, aware that on the other side of the world a committee was deciding my fate. I drifted in and out of dreams until, just before dawn, I woke with the urge to check my phone. At 5:08 a.m., the email arrived: Congratulations on your tenure. The world seemed to tilt. By seven Catherine and my dear housemates—Alex, Trisha, and Jayne—had gathered me for a morning dip in the sea. The path to the beach wound steeply downward, a staircase carved through lush trees where morning light filtered in golden threads. The air smelled of salt and eucalyptus oil; each step felt like descending into a blessing. When we reached the sand, the tide breathed against the shore, cold and alive. We waded in together, squealing at the shock of it, then surrendering to the salt and laughter that rose around us. The ocean held us as we floated, our hair fanning like sea grass, our voices mingling with the gulls. In that salt-bright morning I felt something shift—the armor of striving dissolving in the water, replaced by a quiet joy. Tenure was supposed to be the pinnacle, yet what I felt most was gratitude—for these women, for the years that had carried me here, for the wide patient sea that received our celebration. As sunlight spilled across the waves, I whispered into the wind, Now I can finally breathe.

As we climbed back up the steep path, towels draped over our shoulders, the day already beginning to warm, I felt lighter—buoyed by salt and laughter, by the sense that something within me had unlatched. I didn't know then that this exhale would be brief, or that the next season would ask for a different kind of strength.

When the World Tilts: The Call in Montréal

By summer the world had tilted north. Two months after that salt-soaked farewell at Q Station, I found myself in Montréal, Canada, attending a conference on engineering education—an area that had become my newest passion since earning tenure. The city was all old stone and bright flower boxes, a mix of history and humidity. The air shimmered with heat, nearly one hundred degrees, and I remember thinking that even the air itself seemed to hum with possibility. I had gone for a walk along a narrow cobblestoned street lined with cafés and boutiques when my phone rang.

It was the nurse.

Her voice was kind but careful, the kind professionals use when they must deliver news that changes things. "The biopsy shows ductal carcinoma in situ," she said. "There's a small area we're watching that may be invasive, but the good news is we caught it early."

The words floated through the noise of the city—bells, laughter, a busker's saxophone—but my body heard them before my mind did. I stopped walking. The heat pressed down. People moved around me, carrying ice cream cones and shopping bags, while I stood rooted to the stones beneath my feet.

I thanked her automatically, hung up, and stared at the phone screen until it dimmed. Then I texted my mother and aunties in our family chat. Got the call. It's cancer. Early stage, they think. I'm okay, just shocked. Dots appeared and disappeared as they typed and retyped their replies. A friend from home called within minutes, her voice breaking the surface of my disbelief. "You're going to be fine," she said, over and over, and I cried into the heat of the afternoon.

When the call ended, I kept walking, though I can't remember where to. The world had turned bright and unbearable. Window boxes overflowed with geraniums, their color almost mocking in its exuberance. The cobblestones glistened like scales. I reached the small hotel where I was staying, closed the curtains, and turned the room into darkness. The hum of the air conditioner filled the silence as I lay on the bed, shoes still on, and slept the dense, dreamless sleep of shock.

Wholeness as a Practice, Not a Promise

When I woke, the light had softened. I sat up and wrote a single sentence on the hotel notepad: Wholeness is not a promise; it's a practice. Coming up with sayings to capture my mood was something that Catherine had shared with me at the writing retreat. Putting complex emotional experiences into short phrases encapsulated an inner wisdom. I didn't know then this would be a lifelong practice.

The line stayed with me like a pulse. Catherine had taught us that a single phrase could become a compass—a way to steer through chaos. In Montréal I began to understand what she meant: the practice wasn't just about writing; it was about living. Each breath, each conversation, was a chance to choose presence over panic— to translate uncertainty into motion. What I had learned at the retreat was how to listen to my inner voice; what I was learning now was how to trust it

In the days that followed, I moved through the city as if underwater. I attended the remaining sessions, smiled at colleagues, and nodded at their talk of research and deadlines, all the while listening to another conversation inside myself—a conversation between fear and faith. I walked the river path each evening, watching how the light changed the color of the water. I thought about the body as a system of patterns. My body was sending me a message now, one I had ignored for too long: slow down, listen.

Listening Before the Body Has to Shout

Back home, appointments multiplied—surgeon, oncologist, radiologist. The word lumpectomy entered my vocabulary. I circled dates on a calendar but avoided counting the days. My friends called and offered to stay with me, my mom who did stay with me; my colleagues drove me home from campus, offered to cover classes. I caught myself marveling at the quiet generosity of ordinary gestures: a text that said thinking of you.

I learned my first lesson of this new season: listen for your body's wisdom before it has to shout. The whispers had been there all along—the exhaustion, the skipped meals, the voice that said rest— and I had drowned them in productivity. The diagnosis was the body's way of reclaiming its agency.

As summer slipped toward autumn, I realized that empowerment sometimes looks like surrender. I stopped pretending that control was strength. Instead, I practiced being present. When people asked how I was, I began answering honestly: "I'm learning." It surprised them, and sometimes it surprised me too, how much relief honesty brings.

Healing as a Form of Leadership

The morning of the surgery, I arrived at the hospital before sunrise. The corridors smelled of antiseptic and coffee. A nurse marked my skin with a purple pen, gentle and efficient. When she asked how I felt, I told her I was grateful. It was true; gratitude had become my anchor. Under the bright operating lights, I whispered a silent promise to my body: We'll do this differently from now on.

The days after the lumpectomy blurred into one another— bandages, phone calls, wet wipe showers. I waited for the pathology results, counting time not in hours but in breaths. Healing, I discovered, is a kind of leadership too. It asks for patience, trust, and the courage to keep showing up. My body had become my teacher, reminding me that wholeness is not perfection but participation—the willingness to stay present through uncertainty.

Speaking Truth Before It Feels Safe

When I returned to my Human Factors class that fall, I carried the lessons of Montréal and the hospital into the classroom. The first day back, sunlight spilled across the rows of computers as students chatted about projects. I took a breath, feeling my heart beat in the scar's rhythm.

"There's something I need to tell you," I said. My voice caught, but I continued. "I will have surgery next week. Breast cancer—early stage, we think. I'll be fine, but I wanted you to know because life doesn't pause for us".

Silence settled, soft but charged. A few students nodded, one visible swallowing her tears. "We'll work around appointments," I added, "and keep learning together. That's what human factors really mean—designing for our limits to maximize our strengths."

A small laugh rippled through the room, breaking the tension. I saw in their faces not pity but solidarity. In that moment, vulnerability became a bridge. Speak your truth before it feels safe—your voice is how safety begins.

After that day in class, something inside me eased. The air in the room felt lighter, and I realized I had just taught the most important lesson of the semester—the one that wasn't in the syllabus. I didn't plan to make a habit of sharing personal stories, but that afternoon I understood that leadership is sometimes simply the courage to stand in your truth and let others stand beside you.

The weeks that followed became a careful choreography of treatment, rest, and teaching. I learned to schedule my energy like office hours: mornings for lectures, afternoons for naps, evenings for quiet reflection. I kept the incision clean and my spirit open. My students sent emails and text messages, one student stopped me in the breezeway and solemnly said, "We are all rooting for you!"

Redefining Security and Success

Tenure had once symbolized security, yet it was this season—post-diagnosis, mid-healing—that taught me what real stability feels like. It isn't the permanence of a title; it's the alignment between your outer achievements and your inner truth. For years I had shaped myself to fit the expectations of a system that prized productivity over presence. I had silenced my intuition to meet invisible standards, convincing myself that quiet was compliance rather than wisdom. My body, patient but insistent, had finally intervened.

Now, when I think about that spring at Q Station and the summer heat of Montréal, I see the pattern clearly. Each season demanded a different form of courage: to write, to listen, to speak. The academic in me still loves the symmetry—three experiments in empowerment, each revealing a variable of the same equation. The human in me simply calls it grace.

Let Your Light Lead Through Uncertainty

As autumn deepened, I reflect on nature as I my drive home, moving slowly from stop light to stop light in the craftsman bungalow neighborhoods near campus where the leaves scatter like confetti. The scar across my ribs pulled slightly when I inhale deeply, a reminder that healing and discomfort often coexist. With each step I repeat a quiet mantra: I am still here. The phrase was less a declaration than astonishment.

I thought about how empowerment multiplies when shared. It isn't a trophy to display; it's a current that flows from one heart to another. Let your light lead, even when the path is uncertain. That had become my third lesson. The uncertainty had not vanished, but I no longer needed it to. I understood that light is most visible in darkness, that leadership means illuminating possibility, not guaranteeing outcomes.

The results from my surgery arrived a week later. Stage 0, no invasion. Relief washed through me—not the ecstatic kind, but the quiet sort that hums beneath gratitude. I decided to begin radiation after the semester and to meet each day as both teacher and student in the curriculum of healing.

Designing a Life That Can Hold It All

In faculty meetings now, I speak more slowly, listening before responding. I mentor junior colleagues by asking them what truly sustains them, not just what advances them. When students come to office hours uncertain about their paths, I tell them what I've learned: empowerment is less about control and more about curiosity. The question: What now? has become my compass.

I no longer strive to balance my academic life and my creative life; they inform each other. The rigor required in research deepens the structure of my personal writing, and the vulnerability of personal writing softens my scholarship. Both are acts of design—creating systems, sentences, and spaces where humans can thrive.

There are mornings when I still wake with the echo of fear, but I've learned to greet it kindly. I light a candle on my dining room table before opening my laptop, a small ritual of presence. The flame's flicker reminds me that wholeness isn't static; it moves. It dances. It endures.

Sometimes, when the first light filters through the trees outside my window, I remember that morning by the sea—the chill of the water, the laughter of my friends, the feeling of being carried by something larger than myself. The same motion that cradled me then still moves beneath everything now, steady and unseen. When people ask how I'm doing, I say, "I'm in motion." Because that's the truth. Healing, teaching, leading—they are not separate tracks but parallel rhythms of the same song. The melody rises and falls, yet it continues, and I continue with it.

What I Know Now:
Invitations to Wholeness in Motion

So, this is what I know now:

- Listen for your body's wisdom before it has to shout.

- Speak your truth before it feels safe—your voice is how safety begins.

- Let your light lead, even when the path is uncertain.

These are not instructions; they are invitations—to live awake, to lead with compassion, to recognize that empowerment is less about triumph than trust.

And if I could leave one line for anyone standing at the edge of their own uncertainty, it would be this:

"Empowerment isn't the moment everything is certain — it's the quiet decision to shine through the unknown."

About LouAnne

Dr. LouAnne Boyd is an associate professor of Human–Computer Interaction and Software Engineering at Chapman University. Her scholarship explores how technology can expand human potential— particularly through inclusive design that celebrates neurodiversity. Over the past decade, she has authored more than fifty academic manuscripts and a textbook on accessibility, participatory design, and human factors in computing.

Parallel to her research career, LouAnne writes creative nonfiction as a means of integration and healing. Writing allows her to bridge the analytical and the embodied—to translate the lessons of science into stories of humanity. Her forthcoming memoir, Year of the Mongoose, chronicles a year of profound transformation that continues to shape her approach to teaching, leadership, and life. Through both her scholarship and her storytelling, she invites others to see empowerment not as performance but as presence: the courage to show up fully human, to design with compassion, and to lead from wholeness.

[in] louanne-b-8ba90026

The Power Within

Aligning Who You Are with What You Want

By Chris Childs

"Your unconscious mind is always listening. When you give it a destination that matches your deepest values, it will lead you there — effortlessly."

've learned through my years of coaching and training women, you don't get what you want—you get what you are.

You can set all the goals in the world, fill journals with vision boards, and make endless to-do lists. But until who you are is in alignment with what you want, progress will always feel like pushing uphill. When you become the person who naturally achieves those goals—when the qualities, habits, and values of that version of you become your everyday reality—success begins to unfold easily and almost effortlessly.

That's what empowerment truly means. It's not about forcing or striving. It's about aligning.

Every woman has within her a deep and powerful inner compass—her values. These values are the invisible forces that drive every choice, reaction, and result in her life. They determine what we move toward and what we move away from, often without us even realising it. Your values dictate whether you'll follow through, whether you'll feel inspired or drained, and ultimately whether you'll create the life you say you want.

Think of your goals as the destination and your values as the fuel that gets you there. You can't reach a destination on an empty tank—or worse, if you've filled up with the wrong kind of fuel.

I've worked with so many women who've set incredible goals—losing weight, building businesses, finding love, creating financial freedom—yet find themselves stuck, sabotaging, or losing motivation. The problem isn't lack of willpower; it's misalignment. Their goals are driven by conscious desires, while their values—the deeper, unconscious motivators—are running a different program.

You achieve everything in life because of your values. You earn money because you value contribution, growth, or security. You nurture relationships because you value love and connection. You care for your health because you value vitality, freedom, and self-respect. The moment you understand that values are the real force behind achievement, you begin to see why some goals succeed and others never quite lift off.

When I teach about values, I describe them as the heartbeat of the unconscious mind—the "why" behind every "what." And when we align our goals with our highest values, life begins to move with flow instead of friction. The things that once felt hard—waking early, exercising, eating well, taking action—become natural, because they match who you are becoming.

This alignment is where true empowerment begins. It's not about becoming someone else—it's about uncovering the best version of yourself, the one who already knows how to live her truth.

In the next section, I'll share how aligning my goals and values made losing weight easy, business success inevitable, and living authentically non-negotiable. Because once you connect with the power of your values, you'll never chase goals again—you'll embody them.

When Goals Meet Values – The Secret to Effortless Success

Have you ever had a burning desire for something — a goal you wanted above all else? The secret to achieving goals, they say, is to have a burning desire, an absolute belief, and an expectation that you'll get it.

Then your RAS (Reticular Activating System) in the brain kicks in, guiding you toward making it happen. Which is true... in part. There's just one vital fourth step missing — it must also align with your **values**.

There was a time when I wanted to lose weight so badly it consumed my thoughts. I had the goals written down, meal plans printed, and a gym membership I rarely used. Each morning I'd wake up determined — "This is it! Today I'll do it!" — and by afternoon, I'd reach for comfort food, feeling like I'd failed again.

It wasn't that I didn't want to change. I just didn't understand that **wanting** and **aligning** are two very different things. Everything shifted when I discovered the power of aligning goals with values — a principle from Neuro-Linguistic Programming (NLP) that completely transformed not only how I lost weight but how I created success in every area of life.

Understanding Goals and Values

This is the missing link most people overlook.

A goal is a conscious decision — a specific, measurable outcome. "I want to lose ten kilos." "I want to run a business." "I want to save for a holiday." Goals are set by the conscious mind — the logical, planning part of you. But you don't live life through your conscious mind; you live it through your **values** — the deep, often unconscious rules that determine what's truly important.

Your values drive every decision. They determine what you move toward and what you move away from. Because they operate at the unconscious level, they're far more powerful than any goal your conscious mind sets.

My Personal Wake-Up Call

I had a goal of health, fitness and appearance for more than 25 years! Yet I struggled with yo-yo weight loss and gain. It was a struggle, it took so much willpower, and as we all know, willpower is a finite energy. We run out.

My wakeup call came in 2015, weighing in at a dreadful 165kgs, my husband and I went on the vacation of our dreams. Business class flights to Europe, 6 weeks of luxury holidays, cruises, the Monaco Grand Prix, France, Italy, Croatia and more! Magical right? Wrong! Even flying business class I couldn't fit in the seat comfortably, I couldn't walk far or enjoy myself. All that money – wasted! It was time to do something.

I got focused, and over the next Two years I lost 60 kilos! Getting down to 106kg, and we actually did a repeat trip that I did enjoy! However, once back and in the normal life of work stress and business – the weight started to creep back. Returning to 120kg. not good.

In 2024 I discovered Neuro Linguistic Programming, and the amazing amount of information that came with it was literally mind blowing! The power of the mind, and the ability to 'rewire' your beliefs using submodality change literally was a gamechanger for me.

At the end of 12 months of training, my biggest realization was the importance of aligning values and goals.

When I explored my values, I realised my highest values at that time were things like comfort, security, and connection. Food gave me all three. It wasn't about hunger — it was about emotion. So every time I set a goal like "lose weight" or "get fit," it was in direct conflict with what my unconscious mind valued most. My mind associated food with love, comfort and social life. So every time I felt lonely or tired, my unconscious programming overrode my conscious goals.

In NLP, we often say: "The unconscious mind always wins." And it's true. Until your unconscious mind is on board, success will always feel like an uphill battle.

How I Realigned My Values and Goals

The first step was awareness — understanding what my current values actually were. When I did a Values Elicitation (a process from NLP that helps uncover your hierarchy of values), I discovered that health fitness and appearance were not only NOT in my top 5 values, they weren't even on the list! No wonder I struggled — it simply wasn't important enough to my unconscious mind.

When I finally explored my **values**, I realised some of my highest values at that time were things like **comfort, security**, and **connection**. Food gave me all three. It wasn't about hunger — it was about emotion.

So every time I set a goal like "lose weight" or "get fit," it was in direct conflict with what my unconscious mind valued most. My mind associated food with love and comfort. So every time I felt lonely or tired, my unconscious programming overrode my conscious goals.

There is an NLP process where you can realign your values, using a specific technique using 'submodality change'.

That's when everything shifted. It was like for the past 25 years I was rowing upstream against the current, every time I got tired and pulled the oars in, I would drift back – regaining the weight I had lost from sheer willpower. Now I was aligned, I valued exercise, healthy eating, getting fit and healthy and my appearance responded.

I realised that being healthy actually gave me more comfort — comfort in my body, in my clothes, in my confidence. It gave me security in my future — knowing I'd be around, strong and capable. And it deepened my connection — because I had more energy and joy to share with the people I loved.

Once my unconscious mind linked health to my top values, the resistance disappeared. I didn't have to "force" myself to eat well or exercise — I wanted to. It felt easy and natural.

It was like I finally had turned the canoe around, I was powering downstream with the current, now if I pull the oars in by losing focus, or get busy with something else, its ok, I don't go backwards... I just slow down a little which is fine. I am still heading in the right direction.

In just 8 months I went from 120kgs to 90ks and I am still on the journey and on track to get to my goal of losing 100kgs from that 2015 high of $165kgs.

The NLP Magic: How Alignment Works in the Mind

From an NLP perspective, values and goals operate on different neurological levels. Goals live at the behavioural and environmental level: what you do, when, where, and with whom. Values live at the identity and belief level: who you believe you are and what matters most to you.

When these levels are out of sync, your system goes into internal conflict. You might feel motivated one day and sabotaged the next. You say you want something, but another part of you resists or procrastinates.

Alignment brings integration. It's like tuning a musical instrument — when each string is in harmony, the sound is beautiful. When one string is out, no matter how hard you play, the result will always feel off.

In NLP we use techniques to bring these parts into alignment — reframing, anchoring, submodality shifts, and values realignment. The key principle is simple: your unconscious mind must perceive your goal as consistent with your deepest identity and purpose. When it does, everything flows.

Once your goals and values are aligned, transformation becomes effortless. When mine aligned, the weight began to fall off — not through willpower or restriction, but through choice. Every action felt congruent with who I had become: someone who values health, freedom, and energy. That's the magic word: **congruence.**

When you're congruent, your conscious and unconscious minds work as one. There's no inner argument, guilt, or "shoulds." Just flow.

Why Most People Struggle — and How to Stop

Most people fail to reach their goals because they focus on doing instead of being. They try to change behaviour without changing internal programming. They set goals that sound great — but contradict their core values.

The unconscious mind will always steer you toward what it perceives as safe, familiar, and aligned with your values. So, if you want to create real change, start with values first.

How to Begin Aligning Your Own Goals and Values

1.Identify Your Current Values
2. Rank Them in Order of Importance
3. Compare Them to Your Goals
4. Check for Congruence

This is the first step to understanding your why! Why things aren't working, and why things are. When your goals and your values are aligned, it just is no effort to achieve what you want, you eliminate internal conflict. You stop needing discipline because motivation becomes intrinsic.

The Ripple Effect of Alignment

Once I learned to align my goals and values around health, I started to apply the same principle everywhere — business, relationships, finances, even spiritual growth. When you live in alignment, life becomes simpler, more fulfilling, and infinitely more successful. You're no longer swimming against the current; you're flowing with it.

Living in Alignment –
Your Step-by-Step Guide to Effortless Success

So, now it's your turn.

Are you ready to live in alignment?

If you've been struggling to reach a goal — whether it's about health, wealth, or happiness — it's time to stop fighting yourself and start working with yourself. Because when your goals and your values are aligned, life stops feeling like a battle and starts feeling like flow.

Most people never take the time to ask, "Is this goal truly aligned with what's most important to me?" They chase success, but not their success — the one that's meaningful, congruent, and fulfilling. So before you set another resolution or plan, pause and realign.

3 Steps to Begin Your Alignment Journey

Step 1: Discover What Truly Matters

Start by identifying your core values — the things that make life feel rich, meaningful, and fulfilling.

Ask yourself:

- What must be present in my life for it to feel meaningful?
- What drives my decisions?
- When do I feel happiest and most alive?

Write down ten words that describe what truly matters — things like **freedom, health, love, connection, growth, or peace.** Then narrow them down to your top five and place them in order of importance. These are your guiding principles — the compass for every decision you make.

If you're unsure where to start, I've created free worksheets and videos at www.sagelifecoaching.com.au to help you uncover your true values.

Step 2: Align Your Goals with Your Values

Now take a closer look at your current goals in health, relationships, finances, and career.

Ask yourself:

- Are these goals truly aligned with my highest values?
- Or are they based on what I think I should want?

For example, if one of your top values is **freedom**, but your goal involves a rigid schedule, you'll feel constant resistance. If you value

connection, but your goal requires isolation or long hours alone, you'll unconsciously sabotage it.

There's no judgment here — only awareness. Once you can see where the mismatch lies, you can begin to **realign your goals** so they support what matters most.

Create **alignment statements** that connect your goals with your values:

- "Being fit and healthy allows me to experience more freedom and energy."

- "Growing my business gives me opportunities to contribute and connect."

- "Saving money provides me with security and peace."

When you link your goals to emotional fulfilment, motivation becomes natural — no forcing, just flow.

Step 3: Reprogram and Reinforce Alignment

Your **unconscious mind** runs most of your thoughts and behaviours, so when it's aligned with your values, success becomes effortless. Through NLP and Time Line Therapy®, you can learn to release old emotions and beliefs that have kept you stuck — allowing clarity, confidence, and flow to take their place.

Once you've cleared the old patterns, **visualise your future timeline**: What does your life look like one, five, or ten years from now? See it, feel it, and step into it mentally every day. This isn't just "positive thinking" — it's neurological conditioning that aligns your mind with your future.

Finally, remember that alignment is an ongoing practice. Review your values regularly, because as you grow, your priorities evolve. Revisit your goals each year to ensure they still match who you're becoming.

If you'd like help refining your path or releasing what's holding you back, explore the tools, courses, and retreats at www.sagelifecoaching.com.au. Together, we can bring your values and goals into perfect harmony — so you can live with clarity, confidence, and purpose.

Final Thoughts

Looking back, I can honestly say that aligning my goals and values didn't just make losing weight easy — it made living easy. It wasn't about food or fitness at all. It was about learning to honour my true self, to listen to my unconscious mind, and to create harmony between what I say I want and who I really am.

When your goals and values work together, the result is pure magic. You stop striving and start thriving. Life feels lighter, purpose-driven, and full of flow.

**Because when you live in alignment,
success doesn't feel like striving.**

It feels like freedom.

About Chris

Chris Childs is a Master Practitioner and Trainer of Neuro-Linguistic Programming (NLP), Time Line Therapy®, and Hypnotherapy, dedicated to helping people unlock their potential and live extraordinary lives. With over 30 years of entrepreneurial and business and wealth coaching experience, Chris now brings together practical wisdom, emotional intelligence, and proven NLP methodologies to create lasting personal and professional transformation.

As the founder of Sage Life Coaching, the Academy of Results, and My Big Money Goal, Chris has guided thousands through life-changing programs that integrate money, mindset, behaviour, and purpose. Her signature approach helps clients dissolve limiting beliefs, realign their values, and achieve goals with clarity and confidence.

Chris's own journey—from overcoming adversity to building financial freedom and personal fulfilment—inspires the authenticity behind her teachings. Whether through her "Me, Myself & I" personal development program, "Healthy, Wealthy & Wise" series, immersive breakthrough retreats, or personalised coaching programs she empowers others to reconnect with their true identity and create lives filled with meaning, health, and prosperity.

Passionate, insightful, and down-to-earth, Chris believes transformation begins when we align who we are with what we truly want. Her mission is simple: to help people reprogram their minds, rewrite their stories, and step boldly into the life they were born to live.

🌐 Sagelifecoaching.com.au

f sagelifecoach

Leading with Legacy
My Journey of Growth, Grace, and Grit
By Fisayo Odunaike

"True leadership begins where pride ends; in the
quiet strength of service, guided by faith, and
devoted to building what will outlive us:
empowered lives, awakened dreams,
and lasting legacies."

Leadership, to me, is not a position, a title, or a single moment of triumph, it is a lifelong journey of discovery, discipline, and devotion. It is about showing up when others withdraw, standing firm when storms rage, and creating value that outlives you. My own leadership journey has been a blend of inspiration, mistakes, faith, and resilience. It has been shaped by the powerful example of my late father, molded by my experiences in multiple industries, and refined through both failures and victories.

As my relationship with Jesus Christ deepens, it is the bedrock of my leadership. It grounds me in truth, steadies me in uncertainty, and reminds me that leadership is first an act of service. Through faith,

I've learned that power without purpose is empty, and ambition without humility is dangerous. My daily walk with Christ teaches me to lead with compassion, to forgive quickly, and to make decisions guided by wisdom rather than ego. When challenges arise, as they often do in business. Prayer gives me clarity, and grace gives me courage. Christ's example of servant leadership continually shapes my approach: to lift others, to act with integrity even when unseen, and to lead not from pride, but from love. My faith is not a private matter; it is the quiet strength behind every bold step I take.

Today, I stand as a woman leading multiple businesses across real estate, finance, and logistics. These industries often dominated by men, where competence, courage, and clarity are constantly tested. My path has not been linear or easy, but it has been deeply meaningful. Each venture, each challenge, each breakthrough has deepened my understanding of what leadership truly means: the art of influence, the science of consistency, and the heart of service.

Where I Am Now:
Building Empires, Empowering Others

I currently own and run several successful businesses in the real estate, finance, and logistics sectors. These ventures are not merely commercial enterprises; they reflect my vision to create opportunities, build sustainable wealth, and empower others to do the same. I see leadership as a platform to multiply impact, to raise individuals who will go further and achieve more.

Through the Grace of God, in real estate, my focus has been on creating accessible investment opportunities that empower individuals to own assets and secure their financial future. In finance, I am developing systems that promote integrity, literacy, and accountability. These values I believe are the backbone of any enduring financial institution. And in logistics, I've embraced innovation and reliability as the foundation for success, understanding that movement of goods, ideas, and people drives progress.

What keeps me grounded is a strong sense of responsibility. I do not take lightly the trust people place in me, whether it's employees looking to me for guidance, partners relying on me for results, or communities who see my work as a source of hope. Leadership is about stewardship, not status. It's about recognizing that the higher you rise, the more you owe to others.

A Leader Who Led Me Well: My Father, Balogun Abraham Onipede

If leadership could take human form, it would resemble my father, Balogun Abraham Onipede (1933–2014). He was my first example in life. He was a shrewd businessman, charismatic leader, and a cornerstone of our community. He led not through mere authority but by example. His life was a masterclass in dignity, discipline, and dedication to others.

The Power of Presence

My father possessed an extraordinary gift: wherever he was, people paid attention. His mere presence commanded respect, not through fear, but through earned admiration. He spoke with clarity, led with purpose, and made decisions with conviction. He taught me that leadership begins long before you speak; it starts with how you carry yourself.

The Balance of Strength and Compassion

Although strict and honest, he was also very generous and caring. He believed that good leadership requires a balance of firmness and empathy. He was known for quietly helping people, without seeking recognition, by supporting education, creating jobs, and resolving community conflicts. Through him, I learned that true leadership is about self-sacrifice rather than self-promotion.

Creating an Atmosphere of Effective Charge

He fostered an environment where everyone knew their role yet felt empowered to share ideas. He demanded excellence while also promoting growth. In his businesses, accountability was essential, but so was loyalty. He was transparent, consistent, and decisive. Even during crises, his steady confidence inspired others.

His Enduring Impact

My father's leadership principles still influence me. I frequently remember his saying: "Remember whose child you are and walk worthy of the name." This has shaped all my business choices. It explains why I focus on ethical practices, even when shortcuts might appear tempting. His legacy has shown me that real leadership isn't about the number of followers, but about how many are uplifted because of your leadership.

A Leader Who Did Not Lead Well:
Lessons in Silence and Humility

I often say I've been fortunate to be among great leaders, and I genuinely mean it. Over the years, I've seen many leadership styles, some inspiring, others cautionary. Out of respect and humility, I don't mention names, as every leader, despite their flaws, has played a part in my growth.

What I can share are the lessons learned from leadership lacking empathy, self-awareness, or integrity.

When Authority Replaces Empathy

I once worked closely with a leader who prioritized results over relationships. Under their leadership, productivity was high, but morale was low. People operated out of fear rather than inspiration. It taught me that while authority can command compliance, only empathy can foster genuine connection. Without trust, leadership becomes tyranny disguised as efficiency.

When Pride Blocks Progress

I've observed leaders who decline to listen, viewing differing opinions as threats instead of opportunities. These leaders often isolate themselves, becoming disconnected from the people and purpose they once pursued. This reminds me that humility is not a sign of weakness but a form of wisdom. As a leader, it's essential to be confident in decision-making while remaining humble enough to learn.

The Lesson of Gratitude

My experiences taught me that poor leadership usually arises from ingratitude rather than incompetence, as leadership is a privilege, not an entitlement. All leaders rely on those who came before them. Forgetting this can lead to failure. Each day, I remind myself to lead with gratitude for my team, mentors, and everyone who helps make success possible.

When I Led Poorly:
The Painful Power of Reflection

No leader gets everything right all the time, and I am no exception. I recall one early moment in my entrepreneurial journey when I let pressure cloud my judgement.

I was leading a growing team in one of my businesses, and the demand was intense. Deadlines were strict, expectations high, and I felt compelled to oversee everything. Instead of empowering my team, I started micromanaging, scrutinizing every detail, double-checking every decision. My intentions were good, but the execution was poor.

The outcome? Burnout affected not only me but also those around me. My team became hesitant, second-guessing every move, fearful of errors. Productivity declined, creativity diminished, and tension grew. One day, a trusted team member confided privately, "You've built us to do great things, but now you don't trust us to do them." Those words struck me deeply.

The Turning Point

That night, I deeply reflected and realized I had become the very kind of leader I wanted to avoid, one who suppresses rather than supports. The lesson was clear: control does not equal leadership; trust does. From then on, I intentionally worked to delegate more, empower others, and acknowledge even small successes.

I discovered that true leadership is not about doing everything oneself but about nurturing and enabling others to succeed. It was a modest experience, but it transformed me. I became more deliberate about communication, feedback, and emotional intelligence. I learned to pause before reacting, to listen before making decisions, and to trust before passing judgment. That failure shaped me into a better leader, one who leads through collaboration, not control.

When I Led Well: The Sweet Reward of Impact

There have also been times when leadership came easily, when purpose, people, and performance aligned perfectly. One such moment was during a major transition in one of my logistics businesses. We were expanding into new territories, and morale was uncertain. Many feared the unknown.

Vision and Clarity

I gathered my team and explained the larger purpose, the "why" behind our expansion. I described a clear vision of what success would entail for us all. Instead of highlighting difficulties, I focused on possibilities. I reminded them that every great story starts with risk. That meeting shifted the mood; fear was replaced by confidence.

Empowerment and Ownership

I gave team leaders the authority to make their own decisions within their areas of expertise. Instead of micromanaging, I focused on providing necessary resources and clearing obstacles. Within a few months, we surpassed our operational goals, and employee retention greatly improved. Most importantly, our culture transformed from mere compliance to genuine commitment.

The Ripple Effect

That experience strengthened my belief that leadership is about lighting candles, not burning out trying to be the only light. When you inspire others to take ownership, they don't just follow; they lead. The most rewarding aspect of leadership is witnessing others grow beyond you.

Three Best Leadership Tips

Having led across various industries for many years, I want to share three leadership principles that have always guided me. These lessons have been shaped by experience, refined by reflection, and sustained by faith. My experience with my father and in Christ as thought me that leadership is both a calling and a stewardship.

1. Lead with Integrity, Always

Integrity forms the basis of leadership. It means doing the right thing when no one is watching, keeping your word even when it's inconvenient, and standing firm in your values when compromise seems easier. I learned this first from my father, who often said, "A good name is better than gold." Over time, my faith deepened that lesson. Scripture reminds us, "Whoever walks in integrity walks securely" (Proverbs 10:9). True integrity is not performative; it is consistent. It is choosing truth over convenience and character over comfort. In leadership, integrity builds trust. Trust, in turn, builds legacy.

When I align my actions in integrity, I find peace even in difficult decisions. Lead with integrity, even when it costs you. The reward may not always be immediate, but it will always be enduring credibility, peace, and God's favor.

2. Empower People, Don't Just Manage Them

Great leaders don't hoard influence; they multiply it. Leadership is not about control, but cultivation, helping others rise. Your worth is not measured by how indispensable you are, but by how many others can thrive independently of you.

In Scripture, Jesus demonstrated this beautifully with His disciples. He taught, equipped, and then released them to lead. "Greater works than these shall you do," he said (John 14:12). That is empowerment believing in people's potential even before they see it themselves.

In my own leadership journey, I've seen how giving people trust, guidance, and room to grow transforms teams. When people feel valued and capable, they step into excellence. Empowerment is not just strategy; it's service, the kind that mirrors divine leadership: patient, encouraging, and purpose driven.

3. Embrace Growth Through Reflection

No one arrives at leadership fully formed. Every failure, feedback, and frustration is an invitation to grow. The key is to remain teachable. I often take time to pause and reflect. What went well? What can improve? What did I learn? Reflection is not merely about performance; it's about alignment, ensuring that our actions still serve our purpose and our purpose still serves others. Growth demands humility to admit what you don't know, and courage to improve once you do. Reflection keeps a leader grounded, discerning, and evolving. The best leaders are not those who never err, but those who learn, adapt, and lead with renewed wisdom and grace.

Conclusion: The Legacy of Leadership

Leadership is not a destination; it's an ongoing journey of growth. Becoming wiser, stronger, and more compassionate. It's about influence that endures beyond you and impact that multiplies past your reach.

Leadership is a sacred trust. When rooted in integrity, extended through empowerment, and refined by reflection, it becomes more than influence, it becomes legacy. As I've learned through faith, my father and experience, **true leadership mirrors the heart of Christ**: to serve, to uplift, and to leave every place and person better than you found them.

As I advance in business and life, I cling to the lessons that have shaped me: my faith, my father's enduring legacy of strength and integrity, the cautionary stories about pride and neglect, and the personal insights gained from both success and challenges.

Today, I lead with a deeper understanding that leadership is about caring for people, purpose, and potential. It is a sacred duty to serve others, not for applause, but to make a difference.

And if there is one thing I hope every reader of EmpowHer takes away, it is this: True leadership isn't about gathering followers; it's about creating legacies.

Lead with vision. Lead with integrity. Lead with heart, and in doing so, may you not only empower others, but also empower yourself.

About Fisayo

Fisayo Odunaike is a dynamic entrepreneur, visionary leader, and woman of faith whose influence spans the real estate, finance, and logistics industries. As the founder and CEO of multiple thriving enterprises, she embodies excellence, integrity, and innovation in every endeavor.

Fisayo believes leadership is not about power, but about purpose. Serving others with courage, compassion, and conviction. Her leadership philosophy blends business acumen with spiritual wisdom, empowering teams and communities to thrive beyond boundaries.

A lifelong learner and mentor, she is passionate about building sustainable businesses, creating generational wealth, and inspiring others — especially women to lead with authenticity and faith. Known for her resilience, clarity of vision, and unwavering values, she continues to champion the belief that true success is measured not by what we accumulate, but by the lives we transform.

When she's not leading her companies or speaking on leadership and empowerment, Fisayo enjoys spending time with her family, mentoring emerging entrepreneurs, exploring new cultures, and embracing moments of reflection and gratitude.

[in] fisayo-odunaike-texas-mortgage-genius

@ Fisayo@sitiji.com

[O] Fisayob

Beyond Burnout
The Askara Path to Sovereignty
By Larisa Vakulina

**"Empowerment is not becoming more.
It is remembering the wholeness
you already are"**

I still remember the day when my life as I knew it ended. My husband pulled the car to the side of the road, and my heart knew before his words confirmed it. Our home, the place where my two young boys and I had shared laughter, stories, and daily rituals, had been robbed and burned to the ground. In an instant, everything I called familiar was gone.

What I felt in that moment was not just grief, but the terrifying pull of the unknown. That night, while sitting in the car, we made the decision to leave Russia for a faraway continent we barely knew, Australia. It was not an easy choice. We had built a life, accumulated wealth, and started a generational home. But when safety dissolves, priorities crystallize. We jumped from the cliff of familiarity into an ocean of uncertainty, guided only by the instinct to protect our children and create a life where violence and corruption could not dictate our future.

Looking back now, that was the first time I tasted true empowerment. Not because I was fearless, but because I chose to act from the deepest part of myself, despite fear screaming otherwise.

Feeling Unempowered

Empowerment is rarely linear. When I arrived in Australia, my degree in Engineering and Economics was not recognized. I was 33, with limited English, two children to raise, and no career path. Later, when I completed an MBA at the University of Adelaide, I thought my qualifications would secure me a professional role. Instead, I was told I was "overqualified." Too much. Too different.

Yet in that moment of rejection, I discovered an untapped strength, an inner authority that refused to wait for permission and instead chose to create its own path. I felt a knowing that if no one could see my worth, I would prove it by building something extraordinary from the ground up.

Externally, I was climbing, running an international trading company that became one of the fastest growing in Australia, serving as an advisor on the Reserve Bank's Small Business Panel, and receiving awards for entrepreneurship. But inwardly, I was shrinking. Every title I acquired, every award I received, only deepened the void inside.

That is the paradox many high-achieving women face: the more we achieve, the more invisible we feel to ourselves. I looked successful on paper, but at night I battled insomnia, emptiness, and the relentless whisper that something was missing.

Then came the ultimate confrontation with powerlessness, my diagnosis with breast cancer.

It stripped away every illusion of control I thought I had mastered. Yet, what began as fear became my greatest teacher. It forced me to stop striving and start listening. It invited me into a space of surrender, curiosity, and humility, where I had to face every "unknowing" question that my intellect had avoided for decades.

Cancer was not a punishment. It was a profound initiation. It dismantled the woman I had performed as and revealed the woman I truly was, raw, intuitive, and infinitely wise beneath the noise of achievement. It became the threshold where I began to understand that true empowerment is not about fighting life but aligning with it.

Who Empowered Me

Empowerment rarely comes from grand gestures. For me, it came in small but sacred ways. My husband's quiet presence when chaos raged around us. My children, who picked up English faster than I did and became my teachers. And later, Barbara Ann Brennan, whose work on the human energy field spoke to me like a long-forgotten truth.

But perhaps the most profound empowerment came through my illness. Breast cancer became my guide. It slowed me down enough to hear my own soul whisper. It taught me to become deeply curious, not just about how to survive, but how to *live* in alignment with truth.

When I asked not *why* it happened, but *what it was showing me*, I began to see the deeper ecology of my own being, how stress, disconnection, and overachievement had been speaking through my body all along. That realization became the compass that led me to heal myself through surrender, energy coherence, and the restoration of inner truth.

Enrolling in the Barbara Brennan School of Healing in Florida was the next natural step. Unlike my MBA and Harvard Business Course, which were chosen by my intellect, this was chosen by my essence. Those years of study cracked me open, showing me that empowerment was not about more titles or accolades, but about reclaiming the fragments of myself I had abandoned in pursuit of approval.

When Leadership Went Wrong

There were times I led poorly, though on the surface it looked like success.

In business, I became a Master of Performance, negotiating, expanding, and making our company thrive. But I ignored my intuition, my body, and my emotional truth. I sacrificed sleep, health, and relationships in the name of achievement.

I wore the armour of the "strong woman," believing that to show vulnerability would invite disrespect. That armour eventually became a prison. I was exhausted, brittle, and disconnected, admired by many, but known by none, including myself.

When Leadership Went Right

And yet, there were moments of true self-authority and leadership. They always happened when I chose authenticity over performance.

When I followed my quiet inner practice, what I call "Follow the First Thought", I found clarity. It was a simple daily ritual of sitting in silence, breathing, and catching the first thought after three exhales. "Call your sister." "Rest." "Write." "Finish slides." These whispers, when followed, opened pathways I could never have planned. They were small acts of obedience to my inner compass that restored my power.

In my MBA, I discovered that my accent, once a source of shame, made my classmates listen more attentively. What I thought was a weakness became a gift. Later, in building Askara Sanctuary and THE ASKARA PRINCIPLES™ methodology, I learned to lead not from force but from resonance, weaving my healing journey into a space where other women could find theirs.

True leadership, I realized, is not about control, performance and deadlines. It is about coherence. It is about leading yourself so fully that others feel safe to lead themselves.

Top 3 Tips to EmpowHer

1. **Take radical self-responsibility.** Stop outsourcing your freedom to external systems or people. Your power is in total self-honesty and the choices you make daily from that place.

2. **Trust your individuation point, I call ID.** Your essence is your truth. No title, role, or accolade defines you more than your inner knowing. You are the best expression of this divine plan.

3. **Nurture relational ecology.** Empowerment is amplified when your relationships are grounded in respect, honesty, and mutual growth.

Closing / Final Thoughts

When I left Russia, I thought empowerment was about building a safe, successful life. What I've learned is that empowerment is about listening, truly listening, to the quiet inner voice that knows the way. Thrue empowering is to know the self, deep enough to see clearly how you want to live your life, express your true self and share your inner genius.

Every woman carries her own Askara within, her inner resonance, her divine compass. Empowerment is not about chasing more, proving more, or performing harder. It is about choosing to trust that compass, even when the path ahead looks uncertain.

I invite you, dear reader, to pause. To breathe. To listen. And to follow your first thought, that first whisper that rises when you are still. It may look small, but it holds the seed of your sovereignty.

Empowerment begins here.

About Larisa

Larisa Vakulina is a multi-award-winning entrepreneur, healer, and founder of Askara Sanctuary in South Australia. With an MBA from the University of Adelaide and studies at Harvard Business School, she built one of Australia's fastest-growing international trading companies before devoting her life to guiding women into soul-led success.

A graduate of the Barbara Brennan School of Healing, Larisa created The ASKARA PRINCIPLES™ methodology, a transformational method that integrates business acumen, emotional intelligence, and spiritual mastery. Having self-healed from breast cancer without any medical protocols and rebuilt after profound loss, she embodies the essence of resilience, grace, and conscious evolved leadership.

Through retreats, Masterclass and online 12-weeks THE ASKARA PRINCIPLES™ Methodology, and her upcoming book The Askara Principles: The 3 Powerful Truths for Successful Women to Have It All, Larisa empowers high-achieving women to shift from overdrive to alignment, creating optimal health, authentic wealth, and fulfilled relationships. She stands for success with soul, feminine embodiment, and spiritual intelligence as the currency of the future.

 larisavakulina.com

 larisa-vakulina-7aaa15148

 larisa@askara.com.au

Growing Pains
by Cassandra Carson

"Work like hell and fight for the things you care about so fiercely that it inspires others to fight for them too."

Introductions—whether formal or informal, with employees on my team or from other organizations often lead to the same reaction once people hear my job responsibilities and the many roles I juggle. People usually respond with something like, "That sounds like a tough job," or, "How do you do it? How do you balance it all?"

My usual response was, "I don't know. I didn't want the job—it just kind of fell to me. I was lucky to be in the right place at the right time."

One day, a good friend and mentor overheard me say this to a colleague. After the conversation ended, he pulled me aside and said, "Stop telling people you didn't want the job. And quit telling them luck had a role in it."

This friend, who coached me, encouraged me, challenged me with thoughtful leadership discussions, and explored strategic management ideas with me—told me it frustrated him because he knew it wasn't't true. He was right. It wasn't true. But (1) I didn't know how to accept compliments, and (2) I didn't know how to humbly brag about just how excited I was to be in the position.

At the time, I had been a supervisor for two years, with eight years in the organization overall. Many thought I was too young and inexperienced for the job. Others assumed I got the role because I was a "yes person" or a people pleaser. I also had two young children, and my marriage was headed toward divorce.

But the truth was, I *did* want the opportunity. I wanted to lead, to make the organization better, to mentor people and help them grow. I wanted to grow. I had so many ideas and so much energy that I could hardly contain how excited and scared I was. The opportunity to lead was before me and I grabbed it by the horns and embraced the moment.

Being a leader doesn't happen overnight, it comes to those who have discipline, accountability, hard work and humility. First, I worked my way through several non-leadership roles. I studied, I learned, and I've always worked hard. Luck didn't get me into my role. My hard work to establish trust, loyalty, and dependability in my organization got me to where I am today. I wanted others around me to succeed. Through my career, I also prioritize my family, friends and though I'm still working on myself, having other responsibilities outside of my career helps to build my leadership even more, because it makes me human.

If you're reading this and any of it sounds familiar, I hope you'll stick with me through the next few paragraphs to see where my journey took me, where I am now, and what I learned along the way.

Why We Need to Stop Saying "I Didn't Want the Job".

First, you either want to be a leader or you don't. It doesn't just "fall to you."

Second, other people likely want your job. When you make it sound like it was luck or an easy path, which are probably not true, it frustrates your peers and competitors (and even your friends).

And lastly, if you're actually a decent person, boss, and leader, it's annoying for others to hear you dismiss your role by saying things like, "Oh, I didn't really want the job" or "I just got lucky." What I *should* have said back then was something like: "Yes, it's a tough job, but I love it. I work hard. I set goals. I have a great team. I delegate well (most days). I want others around me to succeed. I prioritize time for family, friends, and—though I'm still working on this—myself. It wasn't luck. I worked hard to establish trust, loyalty, and dependability in my organization. I'm a problem-solver by nature. I let go of grudges. I worked my way through several non-leadership roles first. I studied, I learned, and I've always worked hard. No—it wasn't just luck."

The Fear Factor

I was scared. I was scared I'd fail and let down my family, friends, and colleagues, many of whom were also great friends who were counting on me. When this leadership opportunity presented itself, the organization was coming out of years of leadership turnover. It was a revolving door of people and problems. I was up for the challenge, but still terrified of failure.

"Can I balance it all? Do I really want this? Am I good enough? Can I lead?"

After my mentor confronted me and we talked it through, I quit telling people I didn't want the job. Instead, I started accepting "tough job" comments as compliments.

I've referenced this as the hardest job I've held. In my current role, the day-to-day responsibilities are dynamic and closely resemble those of a Chief Operating Officer. I help manage over 650 employees across more than 12 offsite locations, which we oversee from both a building and logistics standpoint. We also maintain a fleet of over 450 vehicles.

In addition to operational oversight, I'm also responsible for daily HR functions—ranging from handling performance management to addressing misconduct. I oversee more than 14 programs, to include our health and wellness program (full time nurse on staff) as well as our evidence and records management program, I have 17 direct reports within my organizational structure. Managing emotions, making thoughtful decisions, and having meaningful conversations are constant demands of the role—it often feels like I always have to be "on."

Working with the federal government adds its own complexities. Addressing performance issues isn't always straightforward, and the standard perception of a government employee doesn't always align with reality. I work diligently—and, as some might say, firmly—to address underperformance. Our organization has approximately 37,000 employees, and I'm committed to ensuring we maintain a reputation for excellence.

While I hold people accountable, I also recognize that not every team will be full of "rockstars"—and that's okay. I value the unique contributions each person brings. Sometimes that contribution is as simple as preparing copies, shredding documents, or supporting meeting logistics. But without those roles, we would fail. I strive to build on those individual strengths by setting clear, tailored expectations for each employee, because no two employees are the same.

Now my response, "You have the hardest job—how do you balance it all?" well, "I have a great team. I love challenges. I'm supported by my family, colleagues, and friends. As cliché as it sounds, we're in this together."

The Importance of Support

Great leaders have incredible people around them. I'm fortunate to have both. My team is full of strong leaders and hardworking employees. I also have a network of peers and mentors I can bounce ideas off.

And then there's Hannah, my assistant. She keeps me on task (sometimes hourly) and isn't afraid to give me raw, honest feedback when I need it most. Everyone needs a "Hannah" someone in your corner you can trust to call you out when necessary.

I also involve other supervisors in decision-making and seek input from colleagues outside my chain of command. I don't make decisions in a vacuum. Buy-in matters, and so do perspectives I may be missing.

Outside the office, I work to grow personally and professionally—reading, listening, and constantly learning. My mom, after my divorce, became my biggest supporter, stepping in to help with my kids (then ages seven and nine). She's still my role model. My children, too, are proud of me in their own ways, even if some days are hard for them.

I couldn't name everyone in my circle here, but they know who they are—the ones who walked through leadership challenges *and* personal struggles with me. Their support has shaped me.

Leadership Lessons Learned

The three most important traits I've learned to value are:

1. Being a good listener.

2. Empathy.

3. Accountability.

I've learned self-awareness is critical. You can't lead well if you don't know your strengths and weaknesses.

One tip I'd give, is learn how to be confrontational *without* being confrontational. Hard conversations don't need yelling or accusations. The conversations can be calm, clear, and respectful. I've found it easier to have these conversations when I prepare, script main points, and set boundaries. With practice, it gets easier.

Leadership also requires trust, and I've learned you can't trust everyone. My inner circle is small four people who I know share my ethics, values, and commitment to the mission. Find your circle. And accept that sometimes leadership decisions will cost you friendships. That's part of the job.

From my very first boss, I was given a seat at the table and told my ideas mattered. That confidence carried me forward. With the seat came responsibility, and I never wanted to jeopardize my credibility, ethics, or morals. More than anything, I promised myself to always be authentic.

In rooms full of intelligent, creative people, authenticity is what draws others in—not imitation or pretending to embody someone else's leadership style.

Paying It Forward

As I move into the next chapter of my journey, I'm focused on mentoring others—especially women. Most of my mentors were men, and while they gave me opportunities and critical feedback, I often faced harsher criticism from women. I realized those women probably lacked the support and opportunities I had, and that shaped my own approach.

Now, I make it a point to bring women in, to give them seats at the table, to support and cheer them on. As women, we're already hard enough on ourselves, as leaders, mothers, daughters, partners, friends. The change has to start with us.

I surround myself with motivated, positive women, learn from them, and show up for them — professionally and personally.

Closing Thoughts

To close, here are my three best leadership tips:

1. Be your true, authentic self.

2. Take care of others.

3. Work like hell and fight for the things you care about so fiercely that it inspires others to fight for them too.

About Cassandra

Cassandra "Cassie" Carson is an Administrative Officer with the Department of Justice, where she combines over 13 years of cross-industry experience with a passion for building strong, people-focused teams. With a Master's degree in Human Resource Management from the University of Oklahoma, she brings both academic expertise and real-world insight to every role she takes on.

Her career journey is marked by versatility—ranging from program management in the healthcare industry to producing in the fast-paced world of news media. Each chapter has strengthened her ability to lead with empathy, communicate with clarity, and solve problems with creativity.

At the Department of Justice, she thrives on collaboration and enjoys finding innovative ways to streamline operations while keeping people at the heart of the process. Known for her leadership and event planning skills, she is motivated by opportunities to connect, support, and empower those around her.

Outside the office, she finds her greatest joy in spending time with her two children. Together, they love being outdoors and caring for their family's "mini zoo," which keeps life lively, fun, and full of adventure.

 cassie-carson-oktx

 cassie.carson.oktx

Lessons on Resilience
by Alex Harris

"Resilience is underrated!"

Tip 1. Resilience is underrated

If there is just one thing you take away from my story, this is the most important.

A little adversity is not a bad thing. It builds character, discipline and resilience. The ability to get up and go again, set-back after set-back. The story of my life.

This ability to get back up and try again is essential. Because if you give up on your goals and ideas, you are giving up on life.

Stop thinking a mistake or failure is the end of the world. Let yourself make mistakes. Embrace the missed steps, the career ending mistakes, the business failures.

It forces humility, which is always a good thing. It drives self-examination. And honest introspection is the foundation for growth.

Don't be tempted to make life easy for your children. Let them make mistakes too so they can learn for themselves how to do things better; that it isn't the end of the world; that they can and must get up and try again. Even if something different.

I've lost count of how many times I have come back from life-altering setbacks. As devastating as the impact might be in the short term, it is always an invitation to open a new door, and enter the next opportunity a better, stronger person.

Tip 2. Learning is in the failures, reinvention the way forward

If we get everything right, we are forever in a zone of comfort. Comfort breeds laziness of ideas and effort.

It is only in the making of mistakes and failures that we learn how to do things better, differently, or not at all.

It is in the failure that we grow character. It pushes us to be more creative, to find solutions and new ways of doing things; to become pliable, and resilient. To try something different.

Critical to this is accepting, or allowing, that the set-back is temporary. This too shall pass. You will survive.

Mine has been a life of lessons.

There is joy in learning. Excitement in trying something different, in allowing yourself to follow innate desire rather than doing what is expected of you.

How we respond to failure or mistakes, we often learned from our mothers.

What lessons are you teaching your daughters?

Tip 3. How we handle money can be the difference in whether we succeed or don't

Specifically, what lessons are you teaching your daughters around money?

Are they waiting for a knight in shining armour to rescue them from their poverty? Or are they building wealth in their own right?

It really doesn't matter how much money you make. It is not how much you earn, but what you do with what you have that makes a difference.

I have watched neighbours earning a third of what I did at one time, buy property after property. They didn't spend like I did. They saved and lived frugally to set themselves and their kids up for life.

To better manage the money we have, we first have to understand our relationship with it.

What was my first lesson about money?

When I was growing up my mother was a home maker and my father worked for the Australian government. His salary wasn't huge but it was enough to support a family of five, if he didn't drink it all.

I watched my mother every Friday beg for the housekeeping money. While he usually gave it, it was always with complaint.

I learned that with money came control.

We couldn't do what the neighbourhood children did, we didn't have the toys or gadgets they did, because Mum's housekeeping funds did not stretch beyond bare necessities.

Mum made our clothes and cut our hair. We walked two miles to school, and took our lunch - a green apple for morning tea and brown bread Vegemite sandwich for lunch. Every single day.

My mother couldn't leave, she said, because she had no way of supporting us.

I learned that not having money could be humiliating.

When I turned 14, just a year into high school, my father told me he was sick of paying school fees. As the youngest with siblings that had gone to private boarding schools, Dad was now done with that responsibility.

I was on my own. If I wanted to continue at the wonderful Brigidine Girls College in Brisbane at which I had started, I would have to pay for it.

And I did. My babysitting jobs had averaged once or twice a month and paid 75 cents per hour. To pay tuition that ran to hundreds of dollars per term (the good old days), I needed more than that.

So, I went to my clients and asked if they were happy with me, and if they were, to pay me $1 per hour and to refer me to their friends. And then I went door-to-door with their written references, selling my services to new families.

I learned that people respect you when you stand on your own two feet.

They respect you when you put a value on your services. And I learned to respect myself.

It was also my first lesson on the kindness of strangers.

Not once did I earn $3 for a three hour sit. From that moment on, it nearly always was $5-$10 per gig.

Soon I had more business than I could handle and had to get girlfriends to take on my excess jobs. They paid me $2 per job for the referral. Even my mother took jobs for me.

I learned the value of a good work ethic, and that others placed value on this too.

To this I added waitressing at a local French restaurant on Saturday nights and serving cake and donuts on Saturday mornings at Indooroopilly Shopping Mall.

My restaurant clients were often my babysitting clients. And my tips grew, sometimes $10 from a table, and on one occasion it was a $50 tip. I felt rich.

And I learned it doesn't matter the sum. If suddenly you had more than before, the sense of joy was palpable.

I learned the value of gratitude.

The more grateful I became, the more income I earned, the greater the sense of joy and gratitude, the more income I earned, the more goals I ticked off.

My school fees were paid in envelopes of cash, and mostly small bills. It was, remarkably, several years before the nuns realised why.

In the meantime, my father took up gambling, generally losing heavily. He began to borrow money from me to put on the horses. I charged him interest (double my money if he lost) and required payment in full on the day, regardless of his form.

He never argued, and always paid up. And sometimes even took me with him to the races as his good luck charm.

At age 15 I learned that having money could change the balance of power.

It transformed my relationship with my father at the time. I was no longer fearful. He no longer had that power over me and knew it.

With my own money, I now bought my own clothes, went to the parties and movies of my choice, and away for vacations with friends.

And at seventeen I moved out of home to share a house in Toowong with some guys in university, I met through their ad in the Courier Mail. My parents didn't stop me. Because they couldn't.

A consumption obsessed society is not one in which long-term savings and investment activities rank high on the priority list. Especially for women.

Yet everything we can do today, hangs on how well we manage our money.

While women have developed a reputation as better savers than men, the fact is, it is a far greater challenge for women.

As I entered the workforce after school, I learned about the gender wage gap, and the grooming hurdle.

Men can get away with wearing the same couple of good suits and a few white shirts during the work week. Women are expected to have a variety of good suits, blouses, shoes, hose, make-up, manicures and hair styles "appropriate" to her position.

I learned we earn less; we have to spend more.

Thank goodness for "work from home" now allowed in most corporations since COVID 2020-2023 that this may not be perpetuated for younger generations.

Given the assumption that women are the nurturers, and the significance of money to a family's wellbeing, it is surprising to learn that so few women have financial management sorted.

If you are running the household finances and you are saving and investing, flipping houses maybe, or building a business to sell, well done you.

You are in a minority, but a fabulous minority we need more women to emulate.

Because I learned many women are also burdened with a "poverty mentality." Including me.

In her book, Rich is Better, Dr Tessa Warschaw talks about a poverty mentality prevalent among women.

"The Poverty Mentality is the means by which negative emotions directly lead to a negative balance sheet of dollars and cents. The Poverty Mentality is a woman keeping herself in Less - a state of neediness, denial and unhappiness. She may do this by remaining in a bad love relationship (*like my mother*), by sabotaging herself in such a way that she stays stuck in economic deprivation; by making it financially, only to punish herself afterward; or by becoming so driven in her work life that she starves herself in terms of friendship, love and play."

And for some, The Poverty Mentality manifests itself in an overwhelming fear of losing it all; of becoming a bag lady.

And I learned that the mental game, our psychology around money - and life - is as important as the physical game of work and earning and investing.

I am as guilty as anyone of indulging in self-sabotage of my success; feelings of undeservingness, unworthiness, and vacant hope.

Undeservingness is the feeling that you're not good enough or capable enough to go after what you want, and not worthy of the reward if you did.

Dr Warschaw also draws attention to vacant hope and guilt as tools of the self-sabotage in which women indulge.

"Vacant Hope is a term I've coined for indulgence in the act of hoping without hope's positive, motivating content," she says.

"It is longing for something you don't really expect to get, or feigning a desire or aspiration in order to justify and perpetuate stasis in your life."

I learned that we trick ourselves with denial - denial of time, age, obstacles and change.

At 20 you think you are young and invincible and have plenty of time. You'll start later. It will be fine.

At 40 you think gosh I'm half-way there, I have to do something. But you don't. You're too busy with life and family and everything and everyone else seems to be a greater priority.

And then at 60 you realise how little you have in superannuation due to an interrupted work history along with lower wages than your male counterparts and you only have a few years left of earning capacity. And now it's urgent.

But then suddenly you are 70 and drawing the pension. There is little you can do to boost your financial security now if you don't have investments to draw on, whether that be property or shares.

And many don't. At least if you own property, you can sell and downsize, put some money in super and live debt free.

But too many women don't buy property - especially women who have been single mums, or simply single and never felt they had the capacity to do so, and end up renting with nothing to show for a life time of work.

And for this reason, a good 70% of the elderly poor today living at or below the poverty line, are women.

What have you been doing with your money?

What are you teaching your children about money?

If you don't feel comfortable with saving and investing yourself, start your education at the same time as theirs. Just start.

Because wealth building needs time. Start early and let compounding interest and dividends and capital appreciation do the work for you.

In 1992 I married Peter Pan. Seventeen years older than me but with absolutely no idea of financial management, with no savings, no investments, no clue. The drama this created in our lives was at times unbearable.

I learned that financial pressure - specifically a lack of money - is the greatest cause of relationship breakdown and divorce.

Get the issue of money management on the table with your partner and begin to study your options and opportunities and make decisions together.

It is so important that you understand and respect each other's values and concerns around money and financial security.

I learned that doing it alone is hard.

You don't get to halve the mortgage or the bills; you don't get to share the savings to reduce the time it takes to reach specific goals. Such as paying off a mortgage.

But it is a choice I made, and many do, to be free of relationship drama. It is neither a right nor wrong choice. It just is. And if you choose this, know it will be harder. It will take longer.

I learned that with money came freedom.

At 19 I bought my first shares, at 21 my first home.

Freedom. The condition of being free.

Freedom is such an important concept, but few can claim the privilege.

What is financial freedom to you?

Free of debt? Free of dependence?

To me it is both of those, and freedom to be, do, have, whatever I want, whenever I want.

It also means freedom to give, to help the causes and groups important to me and my community.

It is freedom to be authentically me.

I also learned that giving away too much of what you have is as much a poverty mentality as not giving anything away.

It is a lesson I am still learning.

Whether perhaps because of a sense of not being worthy and the guilt associated with undeservingness, I continue to give away much of what I earn.

And I learned that people judge you if you have too much money, in their eyes

But there was a time I was utterly devastated financially and without means for 18 months, without a home, suffering from illness and unable to get Centrelink (because I hadn't done my taxes for three years).

Penniless, I learned that people judge you if you don't have any money.

In truth, most people do the best they can with what they have. It isn't fair to judge. We do not know the journey they have been on, the stories of their lives.

Much of my own story held me in shame.

From the violence of my childhood, through the debilitating roller coaster of finances brought on by my husband, through to my own failings as a business owner, and my own choice of burying myself in work that ultimately rendered me too ill to do so.

I was embarrassed that I'd had as many lows as I had highs.

Someone asked me recently, how is it with all the knowledge and experience you have, did you end up destitute?

It's a question that haunted me in my darkest hours.

And yet it is that knowledge and experience and belief in myself, that allowed me to claw myself out of whatever hole I had dug. I am resilient.

I learned I can come back – *we* can make a come back, rebuild and reinvent ourselves.

Failure, financial mistakes, financial distress even, are not a life sentence.

To every such set back I say to myself, "This is temporary. This too shall pass." And it does.

Just breathe, and get up again.

About Alex

Previously an award-winning media and public relations executive, **Alex Harris**'s unique experience in developing the marketing strategy for premium residential property in Noosa together with more than 30 years international experience in PR, media and marketing, has proved invaluable to clients.

With more than $300m in property sales since starting Noosa4Sale, Alex has entrenched herself as a trusted and skilled real estate agent, delivering solid advice, exceptional service and results with honesty and integrity.

Outside of real estate, Alex is best known for her creation and funding of the national crowdsourced koala map KoalaTracker.com.au, now in its 14th year. Alex is also known as a generous supporter of local charities and causes.

Winner of the 2024 Sunshine Coast Business Awards, Business Services (Small) category, Alex is dedicated to helping you achieve your real estate goals.

Noosa4Sale Pty Ltd
🌐 noosa4sale.com
📞 0412 635 274

I Am Super Woman

...even if it almost kills me
by Aisha Rodriguez

"The solid mountain of our true nature
stays where it's always been."

— Jalāl ad-Dīn Rūmī

It's All an Illusion

Before everything changed—the rise of AI, the pandemic, our political climate—I thought I was built to handle anything.

I knew how to walk into a room and make people feel my presence. My confidence looked effortless, but it was manufactured—a polished armor and the constant need to appear fine. I wasn't fearless. I was performing. It was how I learned to feel safe.

Then, after a series of COVID infections, everything began to glitch. My body stopped cooperating. I'd try to speak, and the words slipped away. My thoughts scattered. Sentences broke apart midair.

It was as if my brain and body had stopped speaking the same language.

Inside, I was screaming for something—anything—to start working again. I'd sit perfectly still, willing myself to reset, begging for clarity that never came. My nervous system locked in a freeze state—survival.

The harder I tried to "fix it," the more disconnected I became.

I didn't want to believe something was wrong, so I kept over-functioning and over-exerting just to get through the day. Smiling when I could, isolating when I couldn't.

"Act normal," I told myself. "You're fine."

But behind the mask, I was terrified. The woman who once commanded rooms could barely wake up out of her sleep.

That's the thing about building self-worth on performance: when the body collapses, the illusion collapses too. Everything I'd built to protect myself began to crumble.

I had always been the woman who could make it happen—until the day my body stopped following orders.

And that's when I learned the truth:

Leadership isn't built on performance or perfection.

It's not about money or success.

It's not pushing through exhaustion or under-resourcing yourself.

If you've ever led while keeping the smile on so no one sees you unraveling inside—this story is yours too.

In this chapter, I'll share what I learned about burnout, embodiment, and how to create the kind of presence that builds legacy.

I Surrender

For a long time, it looked like I had it together. I'd spent more than a decade building my career as a red-carpet stylist—running glam teams across the country, traveling for commercials, preparing clients for award shows. I was creative, ambitious, always on the go.

I was working with an industry-renowned producer, preparing to launch the brand and music I'd dreamed of since childhood. A new on-demand app my team built was ready for beta testing and funding. I could almost taste it—the next chapter, the empire I'd spent years designing.

Then the pandemic hit, and everything stopped. Overnight, productions froze. The events, the travel, the energy that fueled me—gone. I told myself I'd pivot, and I did: into strategy, partnerships, and what would become a marketing agency. On the surface, it looked like resilience—but inside I was burning out.

For a long time, I thought I'd suddenly become someone else— foggy and disconnected. I later learned COVID proteins weakened my brain membrane; it was inflammation. My nervous system was on fire. My brain was fighting to function. I wasn't broken—my body was begging for help.

Although there were times where I felt I was fighting for my life. Shame held me in a choke hold. I pretended I was fine. My confidence turned into severe insecurity, constant effort—to prove I was capable, to prove I wasn't "damaged."

But my spark—the part of me that loved being artistic, connecting, creating, being seen—dimmed quietly.

I was gone, my brain was mush and my personality—- staged because "Aisha isn't home". People couldn't quite put their finger on it, but felt something was off. The more I didn't feel safe in my body, my social skills declined and doors shut. I told myself I just needed a break, but the truth was the extroverted, magnetic woman who once filled rooms with warmth could barely hold a conversation. I stopped returning calls. I stopped posting. Changed my number. I disappeared.

From the outside, it looked like I was ok, but I was experiencing a death—the slow mourning of my own identity.

I was supposed to be the one who held it all together—the successful one, stubborn enough to outwork biology. But some seasons exist to test what can truly stand the test of time.

Eventually, I admitted it: I couldn't keep pretending. So I walked away from the industry that had defined me and enrolled at the University of Florida to pursue my master's. I built a marketing consulting business from the ground up—not out of ambition this time, but survival.

It was my first quiet act of surrender—the moment I stopped chasing who I thought I was. It was the first time in a long time I allowed myself to feel grief and shame.

I Am Remembering

There came a point when I stopped being able to explain what was happening to me—or what had happened to my nervous system after COVID.

The exhaustion, the fog, the unpredictability of my body—it all blurred together until it felt like a new normal I never agreed to. But my body had other plans.

The fatigue was bone-deep. My mind worked in fragments—ideas and memories flickering in and out like a bad connection. I had to write everything down. Recall only came when something triggered the information—a sound, a scent, a date, some tiny detail. Until then, my RAM memory felt on overdrive.

Lights were too bright. Even certain smells or new environments sent my system into overload. Some days my body screamed "abort" before my mind could understand why. My nervous system was constantly choosing between fight, flight, or freeze. My personality shifted—awkward, detached, saying one thing while meaning another. It wasn't me.

It's a strange kind of loneliness—being surrounded by life but disconnected from it. Family and friends thought I was taking advantage of them when I couldn't take care of myself. Misunderstood by an invisible injury. I missed myself very much: the woman who loved deeply, gave a lot, helped anyone, and fill a room with energy. So I started journaling, not to achieve anything particular, but maybe to remember my essence.

Nature became my saving grace. Away from the noise of the city, I could finally breathe. Birds, sunlight, the rhythm of the wind—reminders that my body could still feel something real. For moments at a time, I belonged to myself again. Then one day, a mentor said something that stopped me in my tracks.

"Aisha, you have to let go of control—of everything you think you are. The only thing you can truly control is your breath."

The truth landed, because I was open and ready for it. For years I had built a life around control—my image, my output, my plans. But my body had other wisdom: breathe, surrender, ego death.

That was the moment the perspective shifted. I wasn't battling symptoms; I was battling my need to control.

Survival grew into an act of faith.

Some days I met myself with grace. Other days I cried, screamed, went silent—imperfect but honest.

And slowly, something started to change.

Every time I let go—of the shame, the pressure, the timeline, the illusion—I could feel a small spark return. Not the old fire of hustle, but something quieter. Steadier. Powerful. True.

That version of me—the one who could finally exhale—wasn't new. She was the real one. The one beneath the striving, the noise, the fear.

It was a rebirth I never saw coming, and it taught me something I'll never forget:

It starts when you finally stop getting in your own way.

And to be completely honest, I'm so stubborn that Life had to feed me medicine— the pharmaceutical term is called: Safety— one small drop at a time. And the rebirth? An old self had to die. It was brutal.

I Am Intelligent. I Am Authentic

As stubborn as I am, there came a day when I finally said, enough. I couldn't outsmart it anymore. No routine, discipline, or productivity hack could fix what was happening in my body. Admitting that felt like handing in my armor—the identity of the Superwoman who could handle anything.

The truth was, I felt deeply alone. Family tried to understand, but how do you explain something you don't even understand yourself? The world had moved on, and I was stuck in a body that no longer worked the same way.

That's when I turned to functional medicine. After two years of scraping by cognitively and financially, I began a rigorous program— intense regenerative cell therapy, hyperbaric oxygen therapy, supplement and nutrition regimes, and capacity building exercises for the nervous system—treatments that became my full-time job.

Picture me in one of those hospital gowns that never completely tied in the back, clutching down the hallway thinking, if confidence had a reset button, exposing my backside every morning Monday through Friday would be it.

It was humbling—and healing. I started laughing again—at myself, at life, at the absurdity of it all. Somewhere between hospital gowns, IV drips and oxygen chambers, I started to feel myself again.

Healing looked like small, private victories: remembering a word without effort, my humorous comebacks, hearing a siren without flinching, making it through a full day without crashing, crying and realizing my nervous system is defrosting—finally.

Whether you call it God, Allah, Krishna, Mother Earth, Spirit, or the Universe, there comes a point when life humbles you into listening. My body had been trying to teach me what my ego refused to hear: slow down and trust the process.

All this tearing down wasn't happening to me; it was happening for me.

Every setback refined me. Every quiet day recalibrated me. My body hadn't betrayed me—it had protected me.

It was intelligent enough to stop me long enough to remember who I really am.

The first time I caught myself laughing—really laughing—I knew something inside had healed.

I'm still healing—slower, softer, clearer. The version of me that used to sprint through life has learned to walk with intention and personal power.

I'm rebuilding what I once envisioned—brands, community, impact—but the blueprint is different. I'm not chasing achievement; I'm cultivating alignment. I'm not forcing outcomes; I'm building capacity to lead from embodiment.

Every project must honor three things: integrity, truth, and aligned purpose.

1. If it costs any of them, it's not for me.

2. Success now looks like clarity, focus without force, and the energy to dream again. A stronger foundation has been poured—this time cemented in truth.

3. Some days I'm unstoppable; others I rest. Both count. Both are progress.

That's transformation: learning to build while staying connected to yourself. If you're in your own rebuild—recovering, reinventing, finding your way—know this: you don't need to be "back." You're meant to create from who you've become.

We get to rebuild everything—our health, our dreams, our leadership, our rhythm.

Even if the empire isn't finished, the layers are forming with every small, honest step.

It's about becoming—again and again—with more wisdom, more compassion, and a body that finally feels like home.

To the younger me who thought she had to hold it all together to feel safe, to fight for her own life or her mother's well-being: "You are safe. You are loved. Your heart is your super power. Just know the butterfly that will emerge every time you transform will be even more beautiful than before. I love you muchachita. You are brilliant my dear, don't ever doubt yourself."

The Legacy —
What Life and Leadership Can Teach You

Here's what I know now: a fuller, more vibrant version of you doesn't emerge without a cost.

It happens in different ways—loss, burnout, illness, betrayal, transition, ego death, or parting from something that no longer fits. Many people try to avoid the cost, but there's a cost—whether you willingly choose to step into a higher version of yourself or you don't. Someone could really use your super power. Your medicine. Your servitude.

Everyone gets their version of an upgrade one way or another. What matters isn't what "breaks" you or how hard the truth is to face.

It's who emerges when it's all said and done.

Leadership isn't a title or a role. It's the decision to stay present when everything in you wants to shut down. It's breathing through pressure instead of pretending it doesn't hurt. It's facing what's real—not what's curated—and choosing honesty anyway.

Vulnerability isn't weakness; it's access to an authentic reality. And there's nothing like an authentic leader.

You don't need a boardroom to lead.

You lead every time you tell the truth.

You lead when you set a boundary, when you slow down, when you stop chasing approval and start living in alignment.

I still face hard choices, but my rule is simple: I won't betray myself to keep the peace, and I won't abandon my integrity to avoid discomfort.

Integrity is protecting both—my truth and my duty.

Most of us spend years chasing the wrong kind of power: control, validation, performance.

Then life strips it away and hands us the real thing—safety, by means of self-trust, self-love, and self-worth.

Because the people who can sit in darkness without losing themselves are the ones who can lead others toward light.

So if you're in your own rebuilding season, hear me: You are not behind. You are being reshaped into someone stronger, clearer, more honest.

What feels like falling apart may be life rearranging you into alignment.

The same way my nervous system relearned safety, yours can too. The same way I learned to speak from truth, you can too. You don't need to have it all together. Lead from exactly where you are.

Leadership isn't about being the best; it's about being real— telling the truth faster, apologizing sooner, choosing integrity even when it costs you.

People don't follow perfection; they follow presence.

Everything that tried to break you is trying to build you.

Lead from that place. Lead from your scars, not your script.

Because the world doesn't need more polished leaders. It needs honest ones—people like you, embodied and still showing up.

That's what real leadership looks like. That's how you build a legacy.

The next era of leadership isn't about who can hold the most power.

It's about who can hold the most presence.

You lead every time you choose truth over image, connection over control, and presence over perfection.

That's the remembering.

That's embodied leadership.

That's how we build legacies that actually last.

When we remember who we truly are at a soul-level, everything around us begins to heal too.

Our presence steadies rooms, our truth invites others home to their own, and our leadership becomes legacy in motion.

This is what it means to lead as a whole woman—rooted, real, and remembered.

When women in leadership start leading from regulated, embodied truth, we don't just change results — we change the world around us.

About Aisha

Aisha Signe is an entrepreneur, singer-songwriter, trauma-informed embodiment and leadership facilitator, and a changemaker. She partners with high-capacity founders, leaders, and creatives to scale sustainably and build lasting legacy through strategy, nervous-system awareness, and aligned leadership.

Her mission is to serve in raising global consciousness—offering her influence, voice, and lived experience to inspire collective healing and human potential. Through her work, Aisha reminds us that we are already embodied and sovereign beings. We must emerge.

@ aisha@scaleup-360.com

🌐 scaleup-360.com

in aisharodriguez

Learning to Say No
by Margaret Kelly

"The moment you start loving and appreciating your unique self, it's the moment you begin the journey back home, to who you were always meant to be!"

My African Roots

Place of cool waters Nairobi Kenya, is where I was born and raised. Nairobi has been given a nickname *Green city* in the sun due to its numerous natural springs, and parks.

My ancestral home is located in the western province part of Kenya in a rural village called Luanda (Ebwiranyi). My parents would take me and my siblings from the city to the village to visit our grandparents during school holidays. I had very fond memories of the countryside and beautiful landscapes. I loved the fact that I could walk barefoot with no shoes on my feet.

I belong to the Luhya tribe and it held so many cultural traditions and culture that the community adhered to the letter. I observed and experienced a lot of cultural systems that seem to be very productive but others in my opinion were the cause of lack of development in the community due to their discriminatory nature particularly against women and girls.

A Girl's Voice is Silenced

I grew up in an environment where the man was the head of the house and so he had to have the last word. That a woman's place was in the kitchen, responsible for domestic chores and raising a family. Over the years women have gone through many challenges due to the disempowering traditions like child marriages, harmful practices like female genital mutilation, including gender-based violence and also limited economic ability thus the reliance on the husband to provide, placing women in a subordinate position.

We were always taught never to challenge any idea that we come across that we should submit to them even when they are not sound. I remember not being able to share my thoughts as brilliant as they were at the time due to the fact that I was a girl and girls are not supposed to show their skills nor talent. "You are to learn how to cook, clean the house and wait for the day you will find a husband who will marry you". That was the story that was being advertised for women to aspire to.

The Burden of Being the 'Yes Girl'

Since childhood, I've always been agreeable, some people would call it being a yes person. That was a trait I picked up not out of genuine ease, but as a wall to protect myself, a defence mechanism (or so I thought). It was a way to survive, to avoid conflict and become somewhat popular. This was a behaviour that I thought would make people like me more. Sometimes, saying "yes" seemed like the only way to maintain peace, to stop a fight before it started, or simply to avoid drawing attention to myself in a world that felt unpredictable and, at times, unsafe.

Agreeableness became a mask I wore so well, I felt like a seasoned actress until I forgot I was even wearing it. It was effortless, I said yes without asking myself: *What do I want? What do I need? How do I feel about this?* My thoughts, my desires, my boundaries—none of these important questions made the cut. I had no sense of my own mental, emotional strength, courage, values and resilience because the other person always came first, whatever they say goes, it was all about their needs, their comfort, their wants, their version of the truth and I felt that I had no fortitude to challenge the status quo. By not acting and accepting whatever was served on my plate, I missed the chance to make my voice and contribution heard in order to make a meaningful difference in my life and the relationships I engaged in.

Over time, I developed a kind of emotional amnesia. I forgot how to stand up for myself. I forgot what it meant to take up space and say, "No, this isn't right for me or this isn't working for me."

Seeing Beyond the Labels

This pattern took root early in my life. At home, I was rarely allowed to express my opinions. Whenever I tried to speak up, question a thought, or even simply hold a different point of view from the rest, I was always shut down. I was reminded that I was *meant to be seen but not heard. You don't respect your elders. You'll be cursed. You think you're better than everyone else. You think you're special. You're only pretending to be nice so people will like you. You have a bad temper. You are so sensitive and so on and so forth....*

Being labelled a bad girl was very devastating to me and diminished my sense of self-worth. It meant that I was being defined by negative behaviour rather than my own individuality. I would internalise these labels and at times my childish mind believed them to be true creating a self-fulfilling prophecy, inviting me to behave in ways that live up to their label thus creating a vicious cycle of negative behaviour and reinforcement.

These words weren't just insults—they were bricks in a wall built to box me in. With each exchange, my self-worth chipped away. I began to question not just my opinions, but my very sense of reality. Was I really wrong for simply thinking differently? Was I truly bad, or just misunderstood?

I felt Isolated, trapped and frustrated due to the fact that my strong will and sensitivity was misinterpreted and translated to a character flaw rather than part of my individual personality. This focus on my deficits shifted my strength and capabilities to mere weakness that at some point I wasn't able to see the good in myself making it hard to shed the negative reputation.

Trying to have open conversations—real conversations—often led to verbal attacks, or worse, a storm of curse-laced accusations that left me reeling. I later in life realised that I was going through a form of verbal and emotional abuse. That this behaviour was not a reflection of my communication skills but rather a sign of the other person's immaturity and unwillingness to engage in a healthy conversation due to being bias.

And because confrontation never sat comfortably with me, I'd swallow my pride and say nothing in return. I didn't have the same freedom to speak recklessly or lash out—I was raised in a home where words were filtered through a strict Christian lens, Offensive language wasn't something I had easy access to even when provoked.

The Golden Rule of Respect

Being the youngest didn't help either. There was always that reminder: *Obey your elders. Stay in line. Be quiet.* And so, I did. I shrank. I retreated into myself, hoping that maybe, just maybe, silence would be a safer place. That if I said nothing, there'd be less to interpret, less to criticize. Maybe I could preserve what little dignity I had left. But even in my silence, I wasn't safe. My retreat was questioned: *Why are you so quiet?*

And that's the irony—whether I spoke or stayed silent, I was misunderstood. I was always too much, or not enough. Too loud, or too withdrawn. Too opinionated, or too disconnected.

I carried a *silent* challenge while trying to carve out my own identity, I had to learn to look beyond the label and see through my quiet inner strength. I learnt in those moments that older people should also show class, civility and respect right back to young people for there to be a reciprocal harmonious relationship. it is as a matter of fact to always observe the golden rule principle of treating others as you would want to be treated.

The Radical Power of Saying 'NO'

Learning to say "no" wasn't just about setting boundaries. It was about reclaiming myself from years of programming that told me that my needs didn't matter. It was about finding my voice after years of being told to hush. Most importantly, it was also about standing tall even when everything in me had been taught to fold, to finding strength and courage, to be authentic despite a lifetime of learning to hide and concede. It was indeed a powerful personal journey from insecurity to resilience.

And so now, I practice. I stumble. I still second-guess myself. I am endeavouring to replacing the old conditioning of the ingrained need to please others with a commitment to my own wellbeing. My refusal to be silenced has come to be the expression of a newly empowered self. I say "NO" when I must, thus honouring the part of me that was once silenced. Because what I now know is that agreeing to everything isn't kindness "Silent acceptance is not strength-its surrender dressed up as peace" – it's spreading myself too thin, a form of erasure. Erasing my own voice, boundaries and authentic self-led me to experience burnout, resentment and a diminished sense of self-worth, making my relationship turn into a form of unsustainable transaction. Therefore, I made a decision to refuse to accommodate ideas and notions that do not align with my higher self.

Transformational Leadership Journey

Many years later I relocated to Northern Ireland with my husband and that's when I embarked on a self-development journey after realising how much damage I had to repair in my life. My life has so much promise requiring me to eliminate the limiting beliefs that were set up as a child. To burn the boats and to never look back again. I made a decision to embrace a positive mindset going forward in life.

My leadership journey began when my husband introduced me to the book *Think and Grow Rich* by Napoleon Hill. The man who interviewed more than 500 millionaires to gather information for the book Think and Grow Rich. I embarked on a glorious journey of studying Napoleon Hill Principles daily.

Having had a clear understanding of the quote that says *whatever the mind of man can conceive it can achieve*, I later manifested an incredible once in a lifetime opportunity that was granted to me by the CEO of Napoleon Hill institute Cliona O'Hara, to become a Certified Napoleon Hill Coach/Ambassador.

Napoleon Hill Principles as a Guide

I have since become an avid student and feeling very bless to came across many amazing mentors who paved the way for my personal development journey. The following principles According to Napoleon Hill, have become my guiding light to my leadership experiencing into a life that is now filled with endless possibilities and a peace of mind.

Definiteness of purpose is about knowing who you are and what you stand for. From the moment I decided to stop being a *yes* person I developed a clear sense of who I was and what I valued in life more than anything. I immediately pressed the stop button on seeking approval and explaining myself by setting clear limits on who and what gets my attention. I set my mind on positive information worthy of attending to in the service of myself and others. With this in mind I started setting small goals that I wanted to achieve in my life, giving the goals full attention avoiding distractions for naysayers and gossips.

"Definiteness of decision require courage, sometimes great courage"

I started cultivating **Persistence** in my life as a clear sign of applying faith in action. I would tell myself that I will keep rising even when I fall...I shall dust myself off and try again and again. Life kept on bringing me challenges and situations that would whisper doubt in my ears but I keep on moving towards the goal learning, growing and occasionally stumbling but never for a moment entertain the thought of quitting. Quitting is not an option knowing that growth is not a straight line but the consistency of rising even after a disappointment.

"Every adversity, every failure, every heartache carries
with it the seed of an equal or greater benefit"
- Napoleon Hill

As a small girl experiencing the opposite of my dream life, I had to visit my inner self and venture into the world of my imagination. I imagined that the was a better way to live in peace and harmony, a place where there is sense of community and belonging.

I visualised the woman I would have liked to become, confident, successful and filled with abundance to share with the world around me. In the still of the night, I would envision my higher self living in a faraway land where I could finally be me, free!

All this has come true at this moment in time.

"Imagination is the workshop of the mind"
- Napoleon Hill

Rewiring the Subconscious Mind

Having been exposed to the cultural bias and expectations of how woman is not supposed to express her own opinion and has nothing of value to say, I had to devise a plan that will throw away the keys to conditioning and limiting belief system. I began retraining my subconscious mind with the use of positive autosuggestions.

I started accepting new beliefs that align with my highest good, repeating them as often as I could to reinforce them in mind so that they become part of me. I remember my father once told me these amazing words as I was preparing to enroll for my graduate education studies at the university, he said *"You are a communicator, communicate"*. I therefore use the same words in my autosuggestion in combination with - *My voice matters, I have the courage to use my words to uplift, to lead and to heal, I am no longer afraid to speak my mind with love and confidence. My voice carries wisdom, strength and love.*

Boundaries as Self-love in Action

Saying No brought me sanity and gave me my life back, since the constant agreeing to requests from others gave them complete control over my schedule and my energy. It has enabled me to build my self-respect, created space for clarity and focus, helped me experience healthy relationships whereby I teach people how to treat me by living with my values and truth, it has also strengthened my confidence by taking my power back therefore reinforcing the fact that my voice matters and most importantly it has indeed protected my energy in order for me to concentrate on what truly matters most in my life.

Creating healthy boundaries also taught me that my voice, my truth and my peace are worth defending. Napoleon Hill said that all achievements begin with a decision- and my decision was simple and clear; that I will no longer shrink to fit the social mould for conformity's sake but I will be authentic in my own skin by embracing my uniqueness. I will rise, lead and exercise good leadership qualities by continuous learning, actively seeking knowledge that will enable me to make informed choices and experiences that will encourage and inspire others to do the same.

The Big Question for Every Woman

**The question begs what in your life would shift
if you have your permission to be bold and say "no"?**

About Margaret

Margaret Kelly is a transformational speaker, and a phase one certified business coach at the Napoleon Hill institute and an advocate for women's empowerment, born and raised in Nairobi, Kenya. She is passionate about helping individuals break limiting beliefs, rediscover their authentic voice, and create lives aligned with purpose and confidence.

Drawing inspiration from Napoleon Hill's timeless success principles, she blends mindset mastery with soulful empowerment to guide others on their journey toward personal and professional growth. Having risen from a background shaped by cultural expectations and silence, she has turned her story of resilience into a mission — to help others say "no" with strength and "yes" to their highest potential.

Margaret is an award-winning fashion designer and Fashion Photographer. Her love for music Is her true north. She is currently working on writing and publishing her memoir dedicated to inspiring transformation, self-discovery, and empowerment. Her vision is to light the path for others to rise in confidence, courage, and authenticity.

Margaret is available for speaking, interviews and one to one coaching. She offers online course and a community that will offer you the support plus the mastermind alliance.

ƒ   Margaret Kelly Coaching

@   margaretkellycoaching@gmail.com

◎   Margaret Kelly Madge

The Lionhearted Life
Choosing Leadership Over Power
By Jeanette Allom-Hill

"It is not just about finding your voice — it's about remembering that you were born with one. When women rise in courage, we don't compete, we complete the circle of what's possible."

A Moment of Truth

There is a moment in every woman's life when she must decide who she truly is, not the version the world applauds, but the one her soul demands her to be.

For me, that moment came at the height of my career. I was sitting in a boardroom, surrounded by power suits and polished words, when I realised that silence would cost me my integrity. I had uncovered something that was not right, something that contradicted every value I had built my career upon. Speaking up would cost me professionally. Staying silent would cost me personally.

It was the moment I became a whistleblower.

I did not know then that courage does not feel like roaring; it feels like trembling and choosing to speak anyway. I can still remember the tightness in my chest, the weight of that decision pressing like a stone in my stomach. The hierarchy around me was powerful, immovable, and deeply invested in maintaining its version of the truth. I was expected to comply, to protect the institution, to protect my own reputation. Instead, I chose to protect what I believed was right.

It was the hardest decision of my life.

At the time, I thought it had broken me. The phone stopped ringing. Invitations disappeared. The people who once praised my leadership suddenly avoided eye contact. I had spent twenty years climbing a ladder that now felt like it had been pulled away beneath me. What I did not know was that the fall was also a flight, that the collapse of that version of my career would become the foundation of something far greater.

That moment of truth taught me the difference between leadership and power. Power demands obedience; leadership demands integrity. Power silences; leadership listens. Power divides; leadership unites.

In standing up, I lost the safety of belonging to an institution, but I found the wholeness of belonging to myself.

If courage was the catalyst, then loss was the teacher.

I had spent years in high powered roles leading transformations across government, corporate, and community sectors. I had learned the language of leadership, but beneath the polished outcomes there were moments when I felt small. There were rooms where my voice was interrupted, my ideas dismissed until repeated by a man. There were times I stayed silent to survive, mastering the art of diplomacy over truth telling.

One night, after a particularly difficult meeting, I sat in my car and cried. Not because of the politics, but because I realised I had betrayed myself. I had chosen comfort over courage. That night became a turning point. I promised myself I would never again shrink to fit.

Unempowerment, I learned, is not always something others do to us; it is something we do to ourselves when we forget our worth. From that moment, I began to redefine power. Not as control or authority, but as self-trust. True power, I realised, is the quiet knowing that you can stand alone and still be enough.

That inner shift did not happen overnight. It came through long walks by the ocean, support of trusted friends and the slow rebuilding of self-belief. I began to see that what I had once called failure was actually freedom, an invitation to start again, this time on my own terms.

And so, I did.

The Birth of Lionhearted

Lionhearted Foundation was born from that space, not from ambition, but from alignment. I wanted to create what I had once needed, a space for women to gather, to tell the truth, to lead from love instead of fear. It started small. A handful of women sitting in a circle, sharing stories of loss and resilience. But as those conversations deepened, something began to shift. We laughed, cried, healed. The stories echoed and intertwined, each woman's voice amplifying the others. What began as my healing became our collective rising.

In creating Lionhearted Foundation, I found my way back to leadership, the kind that listens more than it speaks, that builds bridges instead of walls. I had spent years trying to prove my worth in rooms that were never designed for me. Now, I was designing new ones, rooms filled with light, truth, and possibility.

Lionhearted has become my healing as much as it has become my work. Every circle, every retreat, every woman who walks through the door reminds me that I am still returning to myself — softer, wiser, more whole. In holding space for others to rise, I have felt parts of me rise too. The laughter, the tears, the stories shared in those rooms have stitched back pieces of my own heart that I once thought were lost. Lionhearted heals me by reminding me that courage is a shared language, that strength grows in community, and that when women stand together, we become each other's medicine. It is the place where I breathe deeper, love harder, and remember who I am.

The Cost and the Becoming

From those experiences, I created the Lionhearted Leadership Model, built not from theory but from lived experience, a framework to guide leaders who want to lead with head, heart, and instinct. It begins with self-awareness, because leadership always starts within. When we understand who we are, our values, triggers, strengths, and blind spots, we create the clarity that anchors us in truth even when the world around us shakes.

Next is building trust, the heartbeat of every relationship and the foundation of every culture. Trust begins with keeping promises and being consistent in character. It is built through vulnerability, honesty, and the courage to admit when you do not have all the answers. Without trust, no strategy will ever hold.

Then comes courage, the willingness to step into discomfort and do what is right, not what is easy. Courage is rarely convenient. It often arrives at the edge of fear, demanding that you stand tall when it would be easier to stay small.

After courage comes adaptability, the ability to evolve. Change is constant, and great leaders do not resist it; they read it, respond to it, and grow through it. Adaptable leaders turn uncertainty into opportunity and disruption into innovation.

From adaptability flows curiosity, the spark of discovery. Curiosity asks questions before drawing conclusions. It opens doors to understanding and allows us to see possibility where others see problems.

The next pillar is consciousness, leading with awareness of your impact. Conscious leaders understand that every decision, every word, every silence creates ripples. They lead intentionally, aware of how their actions shape others' sense of belonging, purpose, and wellbeing.

And finally, results, not only in performance but in people. For Lionhearted leaders, results are measured not just by profit but by progress: teams that thrive, communities that strengthen, individuals who grow in confidence and clarity.

All of these are wrapped in self-preservation, the foundation that makes leadership sustainable. I learned this the hard way. The drive to deliver, to serve, to excel can consume you if you do not also protect your peace. Self-preservation is not indulgence; it is oxygen. It is what allows compassion to endure, clarity to return, and purpose to remain pure.

This framework became the heartbeat of my work. It is how I teach, coach, and lead. It is how I live. Because leadership, at its best, is not about hierarchy; it is about humanity.

Sometimes I reflect on how I came to lead the way I do, how I found the strength to stand up through that horrific whistleblowing process and the long, isolating investigation that followed. When I look back, I realise that courage was born from trauma. As a child, I often could not protect myself. I was bullied at school and later, in workplaces, I faced the same pattern of power used to control, to silence, to shame. I learned what it felt like to be small, unheard, and afraid. And somewhere inside me, a quiet promise formed, that one day I would make sure no one around me ever felt that way.

That promise became the core of my leadership. I now understand that with great power comes great responsibility. The behaviour you walk past is the behaviour you accept. And as leaders, we have a sacred responsibility to hero our people, to protect them, to help them flourish, and to create environments where they can thrive without fear.

Lionhearted was built from that conviction. It is changing the face of leadership into the future, creating workplaces where teams feel safe, valued, and seen. Because when people feel safe, they give their best. When they feel trusted, they innovate. When they feel cared for, they stay. Brave, kind leadership does not just change cultures; it transforms results. When leaders thrive, teams thrive. And when teams thrive, businesses succeed.

Leading With Humanity and Heart

But I was not always the leader I am today. There were times when urgency overrode empathy, when outcomes overshadowed people. I remember one project that demanded everything from me, tight deadlines, high stakes, endless pressure. I drove the team hard, convinced that excellence required exhaustion. One afternoon, a quiet team member looked up and said, "We will get there, but we are all a bit tired, Jeanette." His honesty stopped me. I realised I had confused productivity with progress. Leadership without empathy is just management.

That moment changed me. I gathered the team, apologised, and began to lead differently. I built pauses into projects, created space for conversations that were not about KPIs but about people. When I slowed down enough to listen, I found that trust grew, creativity flowed, and results followed naturally. I learned that people do not work for leaders; they work with them.

Some of the most profound leadership moments of my life happened later, at ADSI, where I served as CEO. It was a community organisation, diverse, dedicated, deeply human. Every morning, I walked the floor, talking to frontline staff. They told me stories that stayed with me, the refugee mother finding safety, the young person gaining confidence, the community worker who kept showing up despite exhaustion. Those conversations reminded me that leadership is not about directing from above; it is about walking alongside.

During Refugee Week, we hosted an awards dinner to celebrate young people's resilience. I watched as staff, volunteers, and community members filled the room, laughter, gratitude, pride. In that moment, I felt what real leadership is, not control but connection. When I led with authenticity, people opened up. When I listened, they trusted me. When I cared, they cared back.

Leading well, I discovered, means creating spaces where people feel they belong, because belonging breeds bravery.

Leadership has many faces. For me, one of the earliest was Maggie, the Zulu woman who cared for me as a child. She brought warmth and rhythm into my world. From her, I learned that safety is the soil in which confidence grows. She would hum songs while she worked, her joy unshaken by hardship. Maggie showed me that strength can be soft.

Later in life, I found leadership through mentors who saw me not as a title but as a person. Women who had walked through fire and still smiled. They did not rescue me; they reminded me I could rescue myself. And now, I find comfort every time I look into the eyes of women at Lionhearted retreats, women who arrive fragile and leave fierce. Their courage fuels mine. Their stories remind me that we rise by lifting each other.

I believe that at its heart leadership is about finding and creating joy. Joy at work does not come from money, power, or prestige. It comes from purpose. It is found in the quiet satisfaction of earning your success, in the meaning that comes from creating value and serving others, and in the deep knowing that what you do matters. I have learned that the truest joy is not in recognition but in contribution — in doing work that lifts others, in solving problems that make life better, in leading with love rather than ego. When your work becomes an act of love, it sanctifies everything you do. It transforms effort into purpose, routine into ritual, and turns even the hardest days into something sacred. As Madeleine Albright so beautifully said, "Life is about repairing the tears in your community." And that, I believe, is the real work of leadership.

AND EXHALE...

Today, I stand not as a whistleblower or a survivor of systems, but as a creator of spaces where women can breathe again. I lead Lionhearted with the same values that once nearly cost me my career: integrity, courage, and compassion. I have built a life that feels aligned, blending leadership with love, strategy with soul, and success with service.

I have learned that leadership is not about having it all; it is about having what matters. It is about balance, the kind that allows you to hold both ambition and peace, strength and softness, work and wonder.

There are days I still feel the tremor of that whistleblower moment, the fear, the loss, but now I see it differently. It was the day I reclaimed my voice. It was the day I stopped leading for validation and started leading for impact.

Courage, I have realised, is not a lightning bolt; it is a series of choices made in quiet moments. It is choosing honesty over harmony, growth over comfort, and purpose over prestige. It is standing in the truth of who you are, even when the room grows silent. It is saying no when your soul says no. It is walking away from roles, relationships, or reputations that cost you your peace. And it is choosing to begin again, over and over, with grace.

Leadership does not always look strong. Sometimes it looks like tears on your steering wheel, long walks by the ocean, or the courage to start something new at an age when society says you should be settled. But real leadership is knowing that the life you are creating is yours, by choice, not by chance.

Looking back, I can see that the whistleblower moment did not break me; it built me. It stripped away everything that was not real and revealed what was. It turned leadership into a calling and pain into purpose.

Today, when women ask how I found the courage to start again, I tell them this: courage does not come from confidence; it comes from conviction. You do not wait until you are fearless; you move while you are trembling.

That is what being Lionhearted means.

It is living with grace, leading with truth, and loving with your whole heart. It is remembering that even in your quietest moments, you are powerful beyond measure, not because of what you do, but because of who you are.

**A Lionhearted woman does not wait to be empowered;
she remembers she already is.**

About Jeanette

Jeanette Allom-Hill is a strategic executive, coach, and board director whose career spans corporate, government, and purpose-driven sectors. With more than two decades of leadership experience, she has delivered large-scale transformation programs and inspired cultural change across organisations in Australia and abroad.

As Founder and CEO of the Lionhearted Foundation, Jeanette leads a global movement dedicated to helping women live and lead with courage, purpose, and authenticity. She is also the Founder of The Executive Bridge, a boutique consultancy that connects exceptional leaders with purposeful interim and executive opportunities.

Jeanette's background includes senior roles with Optus, NBN, and Microsoft, as well as transformative leadership positions in government—most notably with NSW Treasury, Transport, and as an advisor with the Boston Consulting Group, supporting major federal reforms.

Her board engagements include roles as Chair of Tourism Noosa and No More Fake Smiles, and Patron of the endED charity and iAmbassador for St Vincent de Paul Society. A Telstra Business Women's Award winner, Jeanette is recognised for her results-driven approach, deep empathy, and ability to lead with head, heart, and instinct.

Through her work, she continues to empower leaders and organisations to create meaningful, measurable, and lasting impact.

🌐 www.lionheartedfoundation.com

ⓕ 61565831969221

📷 lionheartedfoundation

Silence to Awareness

By Shivani Gupta

"Life is Short. Discover and Live Your Passions."

At this point in my life, I feel as though I am on a bridge between who I used to be and walking towards who I am consciously choosing to become.

I am no longer the person who waited quietly on the sidelines, hoping to be noticed, nor am I yet 100% sure of myself. Instead, I am in a transformational phase of becoming more aware, reflective and committed to growing as a leader who empowers others.

Where I Am Now in My Life Journey and How I Got Here

Right now, I am in a season of intentional growth. I am more aware of my patterns, my fears and my strengths. I know my passions and what I want to spend my life living these passions. I know that leadership is not about a title and more about how I show up. Show up in conversations, conflicts, quiet moments, with my children, with my husband when no one is watching.

My top 3 passions in order are work, family and learning. It used to evoke guilt in my that work was my #1 passion and not my family. I am the first woman in my lineage to work. Work is a privilege for me. I am there for my family always. However, I am more obsessed about my business and making a difference to others lives. I have a purpose as a mum and wife and also a purpose beyond that.

I see leadership as a daily choice where I take responsibility for not just the good but also the not so good. When I make mistakes. When I have to say sorry.

I didn't arrive here overnight. This has taken decades. For much of my early journey and growing up in an Indian family where traditionally women are trained to sacrifice everything for their family, the first few years of my life, I thought success meant pleasing others whether they are my teachers, managers, family members or society in general. I tried to be the 'good girl'. The person you could rely on. The person that did not raise any issues. The silent co-operative person. I believed that if I just kept my head down and performed well, opportunities and recognition would naturally follow.

That approach worked till it didn't. I did well academically, I was trusted with projects and I became known as someone who could 'get things done.' But internally, I felt disconnected from my own voice. I rarely questioned decisions or proposed bold ideas. I was afraid of conflict, of being 'too much' or of making mistakes publicly. At the surface, I seemed capable but at a deeper level, I was playing small. Partly I had no role models that played big nor was I surrounded by people who 'played big'.

I also started reflect more deeply on what kind of impact I wanted my life to have. This realisation came when I finally took a break from my leadership job and went to Nepal after having cancelled that trip 3 previous times. When I got there, I expected kids to beg for food and money. They didn't. They smiled, waved, said hello several times as this might have been the only English word they knew and they invited me to eat in their huts with their family despite living in poverty. This touched so deeply as I wanted what they had. Contentment. Despite having so much, I felt discontent. And despite them having so little, they felt content. I wanted to know how to move towards contentment. On this trip, I realised that I wanted more meaning and I wanted to help others create more meaning and find their passions.

What I Have Learned So Far

- **Awareness is the only thing.** If I can only work on one thing all my life, it would be awareness. From a leadership perspective, I cannot lead others well if I am not honest about my own triggers, fears and blind spots.

- **Leadership is relational, not positional.** My impact isn't defined by my business or the title but by the quality of my relationships. How well I listen, how I handle feedback and how I respond under pressure.

- **Vulnerability is a strength.** Brene Brown taught me that from her Ted talk. Owning my mistakes, sharing my learning process and being transparent about uncertainty has allowed others to relax.

A Leader Who Empowered Me

One of the most transformative leaders in my journey was someone who I have grown up with. Who did not see positional authority or my gender but truly saw me as a person. My father or papa as I call him.

He gave out sweets as I was his first born to family and neighbours as part of having a son born. This was a time in India where the birth of a daughter was not celebrated due to the dowry system. He told everyone that he had always wanted a daughter.

Whenever I have doubted myself about my career, choice in a partner, buying a home or having my heart broken and asked for his advice, he would gently say, 'Shivani, it does not matter what you have or have not done. I love you. I trust you.'

He suggested I applied for a job that needed 7 years of experience when I had 1 to stretch me in the best way. He would and still asks 'What support do you need? What's getting in your way?'

One of the most empowering things he does was share his own mistakes openly. He says things like, 'When I was in your position, I made a mistake in this kind of situation by doing X'.

When I speak to my papa about being a parent and managing teenagers which is happening as I write this chapter, he shares with me to tell them they are loved and trusted even when they are being difficult.

When we were growing up, each birthday we had to donate money to a charity even when we had little. I would angrily ask my papa 'But we have little. Why do I have to donate on my birthday rather than get a second dress?' He would reply that we still have so much more than many others.

When I fell in love with someone outside my culture and religion, I spoke to my father about it. He told me to follow my heart slowly. He did not judge me for my decision.

I learnt values from my papa which I have applied in my business and my family. Papa's leadership didn't just improve my performance. It changed how I saw myself. I started to form a new identity. I am someone whose voice matters. I am someone who can lead.

The impact went beyond me. Because I experienced empowerment, I became more conscious of empowering others. Thanks Papa. I love you.

A Leader Who Disempowered Me

On the other side was a leader whose style left a very different experience. I'll call him Tee. Working under Tee was like walking on eggshells. The focus was always on results, never on people.

My mistakes were met with criticism, often in front of others. My successes were taken for granted or claimed by him. There was little sense of psychological safety.

In team meetings, he dominated the conversation. When I or others spoke, he often interrupted or dismissed ideas with a quick, 'We've tried that before,' or 'That won't work'. Over time, I and other people stopped offering suggestions. I did what we were told and kept my head down, once again. Morale shrank in the team.

I remember one particular incident. I had spent days preparing a proposal, staying late and trying to answer all possible opposing questions. When I presented it, Tee didn't look up from his computer. At the end, he simply said, 'This is not good enough. Redo it.' There was no constructive feedback and no acknowledgment of effort. I felt humiliated and discouraged and had thought of quitting my job that day.

Over time, I noticed changes in myself. I became hesitant to take initiative because I was afraid of being publicly torn down. I stopped voicing my concerns or challenging decisions, even when I saw potential issues. I performed the minimum that would keep me safe and unnoticed. The saddest part was that I started to believe his message. That my work was not enough. I was not enough.

Yet, this painful experience taught me lessons:

- Power without empathy damages people. Leadership that is only about control and perfection will eventually crush creativity and trust.

- Silence in a team is a warning sign. When people stop speaking up, it's not because they have nothing to say. It's often because they don't feel safe to say it.

- I never want to make people feel the way I felt. This became a kind of internal promise to myself. I realised that when I would have authority, I must use it differently.

He unintentionally showed me the leader I do not want to become. His example became a reference point. Whenever I feel tempted to rush, blame or shut someone down, I remember how that felt on the receiving end. It keeps me accountable to a higher standard.

When I Led Poorly and What I Learned

It would be easy to stop at look at poor behaviour of others but my most valuable lessons have come from examining my own mistakes.

I want to share an instance when my business was growing fast and we did not have enough people to perform the work. This meant we needed to hire fast and people that were aligned to our culture.

I took on most of the decision making and told my managers what needed to be done. On the surface, the hiring seemed organised and tasks were clear and tracked. But underneath it all, something was 'off'.

I did not ask for input from my managers once the hiring started as we were so busy. When they shared that some people were not right, I tried to convince them of my approach. I believed I was being decisive and efficient. In hindsight, I was shutting people down.

Toward the middle of the hiring process, the energy shifted. Managers started to become less engaged, sharing little and doing only what was required. They stopped offering thoughts and the interviews were short and quick.

When I asked one of my trusted people for their feedback, she said 'We know you are the boss Shivani. You're very capable but sometimes it feels like you don't trust us to contribute our own ideas. It feels like you've already decided everything before we even start. Some of the people are great intellectually but not right for our culture.'

Her words stung because I suddenly saw myself more clearly. In my eagerness to lead well, I had disempowered the people I was supposed to inspire.

From that experience, I learned that:

- Walk the talk. If you want to empower others, do it don't talk about it.

- Giving direction is not the same as creating ownership.

- Listening is the best way to empowering others.

When I Led Well

When I was looking at exiting one of my business', I asked for learnings from two other people who had recently exited their business.

They shared generously and then connected me to others who I asked the same questions. They connected me to more people.

This led me to speaking to over 30 people on their learnings from an exit. This not only saved me time trying to figure things out by myself but also gave me insights which allowed me to lead well.

As a result of these discussions, I decided to let me top 3 managers know about a possible exit and kept our conversations confidential and transparent. I also offered each of them a bonus at the exit if they stayed and kept them informed of the values and conditions of each possible buyer.

I asked each of them their opinion on each buyer and I let one buyer go based on the lack of alignment in values. Their trust in me strengthened as a result as their voice mattered and they felt more secure about their future beyond me.

They proactively solved problems, communicated early about risks and supported each other across teams with staff and products.

The result was noticeable. Managers took real ownership as the deal was complete and the handover process started.

In the end, I was able to get a great result for my business and family and I was also able to help each of my managers achieve the same.

My Three Best Leadership and Empowerment Tips

Here are my three best leadership and empowerment tips for you, the reader:

1. **Listen with the intention to understand, not to respond.**

Too often, leaders treat listening as a pause before they speak again. Real listening means setting aside your need to be right, to be quick, or to be impressive. It means being genuinely curious about what the other person is experiencing and thinking. When people feel truly heard, trust grows. This creates space for honest conversations, creative solutions and deeper connection. And my favourite word for this is Shoshin which is a Japanese word that encapsulates this.

2. **Share power.**

Empowerment is not a slogan. It is a series of deliberate actions. Invite others into decision making. Ask for their ideas. Delegate not just tasks but also authority. Give people room to experiment, even if they might make mistakes. The more you share power, the more your team rises.

3. **Model the vulnerability.**

If you want a culture where people take risks, admit mistakes and speak honestly, you must go first. Acknowledge when you don't know something. Own your mistakes publicly. Share your learning. Vulnerability from a leader doesn't weaken confidence. It humanizes you. It tells others that they don't have to be perfect. Just willing to grow.

I see my leadership journey as ongoing ups and down not a destination. I am still learning to catch when my ego starts to take control. When I allow fear of judgment to silence my voice. I am still practicing how to give feedback with both honesty and compassion. And how to balance high standards with deep care.

But I know this much. I want my leadership to leave people feeling bigger, not smaller. I want them to walk away from interactions with me with more belief in themselves, not less.

About Shivani

Shivani Gupta is the world's only Engineer-turned-Entrepreneur-turned-Educator, known for activating passion and purpose in leaders around the globe. Driven by a clear "why" — to ignite passion worldwide — Shivani brings a rare blend of analytical rigor, business acumen, and human-centered leadership to everything she does.

She is a sought-after keynote speaker on local and global stages, including TEDx, and has coached over 1,500 leaders across diverse industries. As the author of eight books on leadership, Shivani's insights continue to shape how individuals and organizations lead, grow, and thrive. Her work spans continents through immersive workshops and transformative learning experiences, and she has successfully exited two businesses.

Beyond her professional life, Shivani is a devoted mother to two teenagers and has been married to her husband, Scott, for 18 years. She believes that life's most meaningful conversations — and breakthroughs — often begin over an excellent cup of chai.

@ shivani@askshivani.com

🌐 www.askshivani.com

in askshivani

Leading with Light
by Apoorva Rastogi

When you lead with light, you don't just
build products or companies—
you build cultures and guide people."

The Spark

After the 2008 economic downturn in Michigan, I graduated from Michigan State University with cancelled interviews and zero job prospects. Through networking, I landed my first job in small town Kansas, the Heartland of the United States. It was quite the contrast from the big city, corporate office life I had imagined—the factory floors buzzed with the sound of high-speed lithography machines and conveyor belts prepared shipments to Midwestern manufacturing facilities. I was a 21-year-old Indian immigrant woman working with men more than twice my age, walking the lines with a clipboard and safety glasses, engineering new packaging designs for America's most historical brands.

Underneath the hum of production, I began to sense a pattern — or a language — in how people worked together. The engineers spoke in tolerances and torque. The operators spoke in gestures and timing. The managers spoke in targets and timelines. The sales team spoke in pricing and promises.

My manager had given me creative freedom, but I had to bring everyone into agreement first... somehow simultaneously to changing the way things always worked to usher in a new wave of innovation. That was my first lesson in leadership before I ever had the title.

Leadership was not about being the smartest person in the room or even the one with all the ideas; leadership was about understanding what everyone in the room needed to rally around a common cause.

After many conversations across the company, I found that the answers to the way forward are presented in the listening.

I then started designing for different client needs while connecting people across departments so they felt like they were part of the creation and impact. This is when I realized that I actually liked talking to people more than working in CAD, and that selling a vision was my leadership superpower.

This was not just the first post-college job, it was the spark of my leadership career.

The Flame

My journey since then has been a series of translations between industries, countries and callings.

From the manufacturing lines of Toyota and Nissan to the product labs of Apple and Amazon, I grew the leadership spark from factory floors to corporate office corridors. I was trusted to direct teams across company divisions, product lines, and supply chains for new product development at a global scale. I traveled internationally to meet with suppliers and worldwide teams, working across time zones and adding cultural knowledge to my skillset.

Every world has its words.

When I started in packaging engineering, I had to learn how to talk in dimensions, load tests, and tensile strength. When I moved into connected hardware, it was about technical features, rapid prototyping, and mass production validation. When I entered boardrooms with corporate executives, I had to learn to speak in terms of OKRs, ROI and DRIs.

Each stage had its own dictionary—as well as its own power structures built around it.

What I realized early on is that vocabulary is not just knowledge, *vocabulary is access*. When you can speak the language of a discipline, you earn the right to shape its direction.

I remember the first time I was in a meeting with the Apple industrial design and engineering teams disagreeing about a packaging change for a new product. The engineers were fixated on tolerances, while the designers were focused on the unboxing experience. I asked one question, about tooling needs, and the energy suddenly shifted. They realized I was not only quietly observing, but also that I understood both sides.

That's when I learned that vocabulary is the bridge between credibility and collaboration.

For women in leadership, especially those in male-dominated fields, this matters more than we often admit. The more fluent you are — in business, design, tech, or operations — the more freedom you have to lead authentically (and the more respect you earn).

Learning the words gives you a seat at the table. Using them wisely lets you change what happens when you're there.

***

Eventually, I moved directly into shaping new technology experiences at a world-renowned San Francisco design firm called fuseproject. It was a college dream come true to work at this agency under the leadership of such high-caliber people with very different ways of thinking of the world. This 4-year incubator-like experience catapulted me into a new level of working, not just at the leadership level, but as a business-savvy professional equipped to head both startups and corporate innovation labs.

Vocabulary is the first step; fluency as a language is the second.

Once you learn the words, you have to learn how to use them strategically—like when to speak engineering precision, when to translate for design empathy, and when to tell the story that makes executives believe.

I learned quickly that this level of business innovation, experience design, and product management had its own set of vocabulary. Now I needed to turn blue sky thinking into revenue-generating products, turn advanced UX/UI into feasible software features, and guide experienced executive clients through new 0-1 product thinking.

At its core, leadership is translation—turning ideas into understanding across worlds that don't naturally align.

When multi-functional teams speak in different vocabularies, ideas fragment. But when you are fluent in a shared language — one that connects human insight to business intention — innovation flows naturally.

For example, business research for defining market opportunities varies from handing off engineering documents for production-feasible designs. Presenting a business strategy to a corporate executive with a defined market and supply chain varies from creating a new business model with a founder who has an idea and VC funding. Fluency is how I adapted to all these conversations; I ended up leading the creation of 14 new products across 5 companies in this short timespan.

If you want career acceleration, join an agency.

The Lamp

I also navigated some of the most challenging conversations, demands, and disagreements during my time at fuseproject, but they say diamonds are made under pressure...

When you lead new product innovation, you are often making a way to a destination that has never been explored, or even imagined. That brings with it a high level of uncertainty, limited data for decision-making, and room for the unknown to become a point of contention.

This is a moment every leader faces — when logic has run its course, there is no clear path forward, and the room needs you to be the lamp.

That's when intuition appears, like a mighty force within.

But intuition isn't magic; it's alignment. It's the quiet clarity that comes from knowing who you are and what guides you.

For me, that grounding comes from faith. Over the years, my relationship with God has become my greatest leadership tool; not because I wear it as a label, but because I live it as a lens.

Faith teaches me patience when decisions are delayed. Grace when tempers flare. Courage when the path ahead is uncertain. It keeps me steady when the world demands speed. It keeps me charging forward in difficult moments, knowing that we have a path to victory if we just walk forward.

At Apple, I learned that design is as much about what you leave out as what you put in.

Faith taught me the same about leadership — discernment is a gift — and creating clarity in chaos requires knowing what's truly needed and what isn't (even if it causes friction).

When I led cross-functional teams at Google, my days often started with PhD-level subject matter experts reviewing product reliability data and ended with executive presentations where I forecasted business needs. In between were designers refining user experiences, sustainability teams running lifecycle analyses, and supply managers asking about margins.

Then came the organizational changes from the multiple acquisitions, as well as the offshoring and cost saving initiatives. I found myself at the intersection of multiple business divisions using varied product standards and incongruent leadership demands amidst recurring business direction changes.

Everyone was speaking a truth, but from different perspectives.

As a leader, my job was to create a path forward, but how do you do that when a longstanding structure was crumbling and the sense of security was dissipating every day? My only way forward was to bring harmony to meetings so we could move with what we did know, and keep walking with one step revealed at a time.

As a woman in leadership — especially as a woman of color — you often become the bridge between disciplines, personalities, and perspectives. It's a gift that is often overlooked or dismissed, at least until an organization realizes its missing.

It takes energy, wisdom, and genuine human care to show up and hold space for moments such as these. This is when leaders become lamps that guide people.

The Light

Intuition became my compass when I stepped fully into entrepreneurship to build my own 0-1 product management consultancy and Web3 company. There were no corporate playbooks or guaranteed outcomes, only vision and conviction. I found that when I led from faith and alignment—not pressure and timelines—the right people and opportunities appeared without all my planning and searching for answers. Simple networking events started leading to timely conversations, and impromptu projects led me to grow skills that now uniquely position me.

To follow your intuition isn't to follow whims; there is a difference between impulses or trialing versus the guidance you feel from within your body. Intuition is following centuries' old wisdom that we know to be true today—the still, small voice that knows what data and economics can't explain.

In a world obsessed with noise, this inner signal is the way to stay connected to what God has called you for. Guard it. Trust it. And let it guide your next step.

"Your word is a lamp to my feet and a light to my path."

- Psalm 119:105 ESV

The Language of Light

Looking back now, I see my journey as a conversation between worlds—from manufacturing to product creation, and business formation to executive management.

Each chapter taught me a different language. Each season revealed a new layer of my voice. And through it all, light was the constant that illuminated the right next step, even when I couldn't see the whole path and family criticized my decisions.

There were years when I questioned if my compassion made me less "corporate." If my calmness made me too "soft", and if my Indian American upbringing made me too "different."

But when you lead from truth, you realize that difference is not dissonance, it's depth from standing on a firm foundation.

Leading with light means leading with humility when the world celebrates arrogance. It means choosing understanding over urgency. It means using your success not as a spotlight for yourself, but as a lamp for others to start walking on the path with you.

Faith

Faith has changed how I define success.

Early in my career, success meant recognition—a product in stores, a brand name, or a promotion. Now it means alignment: peace in my purpose, integrity in the products I touch, and joy in the people I get to lead.

I no longer pray for outcomes.

I pray for discernment to know when to keep the status quo to protect people, or when to push for innovation to grow people.

I pray for guidance on paths forward—not to unblock product success—but to unblock people success, because the rest will follow.

I pray for wisdom to know what's mine to carry and what's not mine to hold for others, because the truth is also that leaders hold blame for anything and everything since they are at the start of the race.

That's the kind of leadership that builds more than careers, it sharpens character and builds people.

This is why I want women everywhere—especially women of faith—to know: *your values are not a liability in leadership.* They're your gift and superpower.

You don't have to "be like a man", compete, or harden your heart to lead. You just have to *stay rooted in grace and walk with the confidence of a victory.*

Passing the Torch

Throughout my career, I've carried one consistent goal: to turn complexity into clarity, and vision into reality.

I've also carried something more personal — a responsibility to the women coming after me. Because when you're one of the few women, one of the few immigrants, one of the few voices of faith or intuition in a data-driven world, you realize that your presence alone can make the invisible visible.

I've had to learn to navigate cultures and vocabularies that were not built with me in mind — engineering jargon, Silicon Valley slang, startup bravado, executive shorthand. Each environment spoke its own dialect, and understanding it was like decoding a new country.

Now I see that each step of my journey was opening up to a bigger and better version of myself and how I speak into the world. Each exercise was building my strength for the marathon of career impact.

So, I share this with you as we run this Olympic Leadership race together:

Learn the vocabulary — because knowledge gives you confidence.
Speak the language — because communication builds connection.
Stay grounded in who you are — because authenticity sustains your light when the world dims it.

You lead from the overflow of who you are.

Every meeting you walk into, every problem you solve, every team you guide — you have the chance to be someone's first experience of light in leadership.

That's what the world needs right now. Be a light.

The Heart of It All

The first word that people often use to describe me is ambitious. Guarding my heart and mind in my faith has brought the peace that surpasses all understanding to the ambition.

Because leadership isn't a performance, it's reflection.

If I strip everything back — the titles, the network, the launches — my leading principle is that I want people to feel more empowered after we've worked together. Success to me is seeing the journey of a new business venture producing fruit through its people and its products.

The world teaches us to chase money, power and visibility, but we do not follow the ways of the world. In fact, the most powerful leaders I've seen are on Sundays, often invisible — their influence woven quietly through the communities they've lifted and the lives they've touched.

This is why I can walk through a corporate office, a startup accelerator, or a design studio today and still feel the same awe I did at 21. The same hum of potential. The same sense that *creation — whether of products or people — is a spirit-led calling.*

To the women reading this, know this:

You were not chosen by accident; you were planted with intention.

You were always enough, but you need to equip yourself. Learn the words.

Be bold.

But never forget the source of your voice; leading with light isn't about having all the answers...

**It's about believing that even in the unknown,
*you are guided.***

About Apoorva

Apoorva Rastogi is a product innovator and visionary leader who believes in building with both head and heart. Her career has spanned continents and industries — from factory floors to design studios to corporate boardrooms — always guided by one purpose: to lead with light.

She has shaped products and cultures at Apple, Amazon, Google, and the award-winning design firm fuseproject, where she learned that language is the bridge between creativity and commerce. Today, as the founder of 333 Polaris Design and creator of the Web3 platform AURUM, she continues to explore how technology can connect people, places, and purpose.

Apoorva's approach blends design thinking with spiritual grounding. She believes that innovation is not only about what we make, but also about how we lead — with clarity, courage and conviction in what truly matters.

"When you lead with light, you don't just build products or companies—you build cultures and guide people."

in apoorvarastogi

@ 333polarisdesign@gmail.com

X @333polaris

Unmasked

Your Journey to Authentic Leadership

By Julie Cass

**"The greatest work you'll ever do
is the work within."**

Have you ever been afraid of the quiet voice inside you, the one asking you to make a change?

The voice that whispers when everything on the outside looks "successful," yet something on the inside feels off. The voice that asks uncomfortable questions like *Is this really my life? Is this who I am? Is this what fulfillment is supposed to feel like?*

Have you ever ignored that voice because listening to it felt too scary?

So instead, you pushed through and stayed busy. You told yourself you should be happy and grateful.

That voice, your intuition, your heart, your truth never stops speaking. But the longer we ignore it, the louder the consequences become.

This chapter is not just my story. It's an invitation.

An invitation to listen. To unmask. And to redefine success from the inside out.

Back in 2002, my life looked exactly the way success was supposed to look.

I had just moved into my dream home. I was four years married. I had spent the last year running my first real business in my first true leadership role, and by every external measure, I was winning. We had exceeded financial goals, earned five-star customer service ratings, and built what looked like a thriving operation.

Yet one evening, standing alone in my kitchen, a quiet and unsettling truth surfaced.

I wasn't happy.

What made that realization even more frightening was that I felt I should be happy. I had everything I had been taught to want. Facing my sadness felt selfish, ungrateful, even disloyal to the life I had built.

I told myself, "Ignore the voice and keep going". But the sadness didn't go away, it got louder in the quiet.

That was my first rock-bottom moment. Not because something fell apart externally, but because I was afraid to look honestly at my own inner world. I had never been taught to put my happiness first. I had been taught to perform. To please. To sacrifice.

And deep down, I knew that if I listened to that truth, it would rock the boat.

Wearing the Mask

To give some context here, just a year earlier, I had taken on the responsibility of opening a 10,000-square-foot spa and wellness centre as part of my family's resort; a $3-million expansion and a major leadership opportunity. I was in my mid-twenties, leading more than fifty people, many of whom were older and more experienced than me.

I didn't know the term *imposter syndrome* back then - I just knew I felt like I had to prove myself every single day.

During construction, I spent long hours at the resort learning ordering systems, designing menus, selecting equipment, planning layouts. My evenings were spent in esthetics school, earning certification. I was working seven days a week for an entire year.

Looking back, I understand why I operated that way.

My parents were immigrants to Canada who arrived with nothing and built everything through relentless hard work, often putting their personal needs last. Sacrifice wasn't optional, it was the norm. Growing up, while my friends spent weekends at family dinners or social events, I worked at our banquet hall. Rest wasn't modeled. Emotional awareness wasn't discussed.

What was modeled was this: Put it in tenth gear. Figure it out. Push harder.

That belief system became my mask.

And the thing about masks is that they work until they don't.

As the business grew, so did my disconnection. I delivered results, but I never felt like I could take a break. I became so disconnected from myself, my emotional body. My perspective was so out of balance, my focus was on my career success. I missed what was important in life - the little blessings, connection to myself and others. The irony is that I was running a wellness center, and yet I was unwell. I was promoting relaxation, yet I didn't feel safe to relax for myself. This led to my bottom; this was not sustainable.

Rock Bottom: Fear and Truth

When I finally voiced my desire for change, to leave my marriage and my job, the reaction from friends and family was shock and a lot of judgement.

"Why would you want to change anything?"

"Your life is perfect."

And on the outside, I guess it did look that way.

That's what made the truth so lonely.

I felt fear. Fear of disappointing others. Fear of seeming ungrateful. Fear of choosing myself when I had been taught to serve others. I see this now in so many of the women I work with: the fear that living in authenticity will disrupt the expectations set around us.

In finding my authentic self, I learned a lot. Here is what I know to be true now: **It is not our job to make others happy.** When we choose our truth, our joy, and our alignment, we don't create less impact, we create more. Our capacity to serve others increases. My first book titled "Me First" is all about this concept.

That moment standing between sadness and the courage to listen to my heart cracked me open. It was the beginning of a spiritual awakening (though at the time it felt more like an identity crisis).

I knew something had to change.

Same Pattern, New Place

Like many people searching for answers, one of the first things I did was change my environment.

I moved to California to help open and run a spa, yoga studio, and salon for a visionary woman who trusted me with her business. Construction began. Deadlines loomed. And suddenly, the old familiar feelings returned even though I had more experience this time and was much more efficient in setting up the business. All this didn't matter because my internal programs were still outdated.

This was my mirror moment: **You take you with you everywhere you go.**

Change your environment all you want - your inner world follows.

That realization was the beginning of a different kind of leadership. One rooted not in performance, but in identity.

I had to ask myself - Who was I, really? What did I stand for? What did authentic leadership look like for me?

Fortunately, this time, I noticed the pattern sooner and recognized that whatever I did this time needed to be different.

I remember saying to a friend, *"I hate this feeling"*.

And he said something simple but life-changing: *"Set micro-goals. Work toward balance instead of constantly hustling and proving."*

That advice helped me separate *commitment from self-sacrifice*. Leadership will always have seasons of intensity. What's important is identifying whether the intensity is temporary or constant and normalized.

Once I realized this, I turned inward instead of outward for answers. I studied the mind: the conscious, the subconscious, and the energetic patterns that shape our behaviour. I learned how beliefs quietly run our lives beneath the surface. How trauma and conditioning masquerade as personality. How the stories we inherit become the ceilings we live under.

From this inflection, the most liberating thing I learned about how our mind works is this:

What had been wired into me could be rewired.
What I had accepted as my story, could be re-written.
My worth didn't need to be earned, proved, or justified.
It needed to be *embraced*.

That realization marked a turning point.

A Decade of Lessons

Within a year, I had begun finding a healthy balance. I enjoyed my job. I had now opened and set the spa up for success while enjoying the amazing weather in sunny California. From here, I was ready to continue leaning into my authentic self. I decided to return home and start my own business. With new clarity and a sense of authentic-self, I moved back to Canada and opened a consulting practice - advising spa and wellness businesses across North America. Over the next ten years, I had a front-row seat to leadership - the best of it and the worst of it.

Patterns emerged quickly:

- Happy leaders built energized teams

- Healthy leaders created resilient cultures

- Leaders who genuinely cared inspired loyalty and performance

- Leaders who were unpredictable created fear

- Leaders who wore masks could not build trust

These insights became the foundation of **The Heart-Centered Leader** long before I ever wrote the book.

The Return - As A New Women

Years later and just months after my youngest child was born, my parents hit a crisis with the family business and they needed my help. I was called in to run the entire resort, not just the spa.

The old me would have rushed in with adrenaline and savior energy. But the new me had boundaries.

Clarity.
Values.

I said yes but with conditions. As a mother of young children, family was my priority. I would not sacrifice them or myself for the business. I would return only if I could lead *my way,* with authenticity, alignment, and emotional intelligence.

I negotiated a four-day workweek.

No one had ever believed it was possible to run the business that way. Past GMs had worked six days a week, long hours, and still struggled.

I held firm: "Measure my results, not my hours."

And the results came.

Over the next eight years, we grew the business 40% year after year. We added a 20,000-square-foot winery. We hit record numbers in every department. We did what people said couldn't be done.

Here's the truth of how:

- **I put energy and wellness first.** Movement, nourishment, mindset it all mattered.

- **I worked with intention, not exhaustion.** Productivity, not busyness.

- **I re-anchored our mission and identity.** We rediscovered who we were.

- **I focused on growth opportunities.** Strategic, intentional expansion.

- **I placed people in their zones of genius.** Alignment creates momentum.

- **I recognized wins and encouraged growth.** People bloom when seen.

- **I empowered leaders.** Ownership replaces dependence.

- **I led with heart.** Authenticity creates safety.

- **I practiced an abundance mindset.** If you believe in possibility, you create it.

And at home, I was present. Dinner with my family. Connection. Love. Rest. I no longer lived in survival mode, I lived in alignment.

This was not to say it was always easy and I always got it right. I didn't and I recognized that part of being a leader is being human and that life means learning is evergreen.

I had to make tough decisions to see real improvement. I restructured. I overhauled major roles and components of the business. One of my toughest moments was letting go of my Sales Director who had been with us for ten years.

One of the quiet traps of leadership is confusing loyalty with effectiveness.

Kindness in leadership doesn't mean ignoring tough decisions.

Letting her go was difficult. The transition was uncomfortable. But eventually, I promoted from within and stayed closely connected to the team. We restructured compensation plans, focused on mindset, and created an environment of psychological safety.

Then, something remarkable happened.

The sales team began believing in themselves.

They brought in record numbers they themselves couldn't believe. Not because of me, but because of the environment we created. An environment where effort mattered. Where learning was encouraged. Where people didn't have to get it right every time or push themselves to the brink to feel valued.

That is heart-centered leadership.

Although there were many highs, running a resort with over 350 staff kept me on my toes.

We had a lot of unpredictable moments like floods hours before a wedding, fire alarms in the middle of the night in -20 degrees Celsius with a hotel full of guests, septic system failures and staffing shortages to name a few

There were days I cried on the drive to work.

And there were days I coached myself through fear:
"You've got this."
"This is temporary."
"The answer will come."

Leadership isn't about avoiding chaos, it's about regulating yourself within it. When leaders remain grounded, others feel safe. I learned to trust the universe and work with its laws. What we fear expands. What we focus on grows. Healing scarcity and fear-based thinking changed every area of my life.

I no longer felt alone. I felt guided.

The Whisper of a New Calling

In 2017, everything was thriving. Our resort was booming. Our winery had won awards. Our team was strong. Everything looked perfect.

But inside, a whisper began to rise:

"Julie... is this your dream? Or just what you're good at?"

I knew now not to ignore that inner voice. My intuition told me something essential

I was great at this work, but it wasn't my purpose.

My siblings and I encouraged my parents to consider selling. It wasn't an easy decision; they imagined passing the business down to their grandchildren. But the truth within me was unwavering. We were meant to sell the business and time was of the essence.

We listed the resort. One offer came. We accepted. We closed the sale in March 2019.

One year later, COVID shut down our entire industry. That whisper saved us.

It taught me something vital: **Intuition is legacy.** And when you follow it, it leads you exactly where you're meant to go.

Stepping Into My Truth

During the transition out of the business, I earned my mastery coaching certification, then my Master EFT designation, followed by advanced certifications in hypnotherapy.

I founded The Positive Change because I finally understood something:

My mission is bigger than me.

It's bigger than titles, roles, or buildings.

It's about awakening people to their power, their worth, and their inner world, the place where all transformation begins. As a coach, keynote speaker and healer, I get to witness this transformation every day.

I anchor myself in gratitude. I love what I do. I love who I get to serve. And I love that my work reflects my truth. After years of wearing masks, I finally feel at home in myself.

Reflection Exercise: Removing the Masks

To lead authentically, begin with yourself. The thing I learned on my journey is that when we hit pause, and do the inner work we bring a level of consciousness to our own actions. Awareness gives you a door to walk through, an invitation to upgrade what is no longer serving you.

I invite you to take a moment and answer the following questions.

1. **What masks are you wearing?** Where are you pretending? Shrinking? Overachieving? Performing?

2. **What parts of you feel out of alignment?** Where do you abandon your truth to belong?

3. **What are three authentic things about you** that make you proud, powerful, and uniquely you? Learning to celebrate ourselves first, helps us celebrate others.

That's the place to lead from.

Three Leadership Tips I Now Know to Be True

If I could look back in time and speak to my younger self in the beginning of her leadership journey, I would tell her the following three things:

1. You are enough as you are.

Say it until you believe it. Worthiness is the fuel of authentic leadership.

It's important to remember that you are unique. No one ever has walked in your shoes or has the experience you have. Hone in on your uniqueness, your gift instead of trying to fit a mold. Keep a growth mindset to always evolve but from a place of expansion versus trying to be someone you are not.

2. The more I care for my emotional and physical well-being, the more I can lead others.

Self-leadership is not selfish, it is the foundation of sustainable success. Your energy is your biggest impact. It's your legacy. When you take care of your energy first and learn to protect it, nourish it and raise your vibration daily, you will not only work from a palace of alignment and flow but elevate those around you. You become magnetic.

3. Leadership is a growth journey. We rise together

The more confident I am in myself, the more clearly, I see the potential in others. True leadership begins within - by becoming aware of the internal messages that no longer serve us and releasing self-deprecating beliefs.

When you learn to champion yourself, you gain the capacity to champion others. Believing in yourself is your greatest power. Believing in others is your greatest leadership gift.

Coming Home to Yourself

My journey has taught me that leadership is not about titles or hours worked or achievements stacked. It is about truth. It is about peeling back the layers of conditioning, expectation, and fear until you return home to yourself.

When you unmask, you don't lose anything.

You gain everything.

Because the world doesn't need more perfect leaders. It needs more **authentic** ones, leaders willing to own their story, honour their worth, and lead from the inside out.

And that journey?

It begins with you.

About Julie

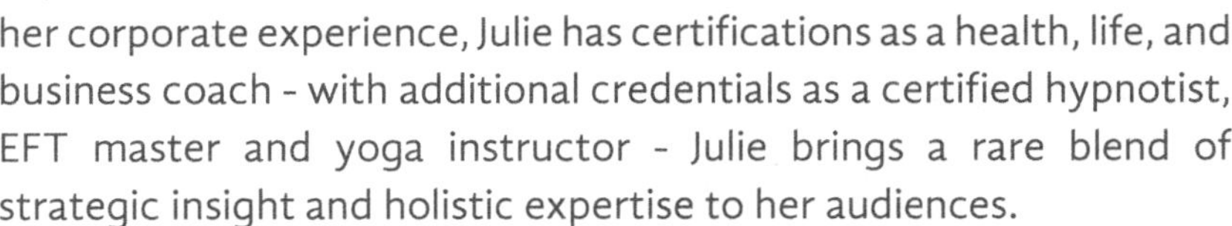

Julie Cass is a dynamic keynote speaker, multiple best-selling author, and recognized authority in wellness-based leadership. As former CEO of a multimillion-dollar business venture and life-long entrepreneur, Julie brings over 20 years of energetic real-life experience to her audiences. Complementing her corporate experience, Julie has certifications as a health, life, and business coach - with additional credentials as a certified hypnotist, EFT master and yoga instructor - Julie brings a rare blend of strategic insight and holistic expertise to her audiences.

Her insights have been featured across major TV networks and leading print publications, where she's known for her ability to simplify success and spark breakthrough moments.

Julie is the best-selling author of *Me First and The Heart-Centered Leader*, two powerful works that explore how high performance and personal well-being can successfully coexist. Whether she's guiding entrepreneurs to the next level or empowering executives to lead with authenticity, Julie's message is clear: when you master your mindset, you master your results.

ƒ thepositivechangegroup

in thejuliecass

🌐 www.thepositivechange.com

The Peace I Built

My Journey to Self-Worth, Self-Love and Empowerment

By Jayne Hansford

"Empowerment begins the precise moment
a woman chooses herself."

When I was asked to recount a time in my life when, as a woman, I felt empowered, my answer without hesitation was: "Right now." At 58 years old, a divorced single woman with three adult children, I have never felt so sure of myself, courageous, authentic, independent, strong — mentally and physically.

In the evenings it is my practice to take time to reflect and give gratitude for the people and events that shaped the last 24 hours. As I reflected on my day, the spontaneous response that had rushed out of me without pause intrigued me and inspired me to take time to reflect more deeply. How did I get here? What was the "work"? What were the lessons? With eyes wide open, I felt compelled to honour my journey and undertake this examination of self.

Disempowered

To play on the title of this book, "EmpowHer", my journey is one from disHimpowerment to EmpowHer. I existed in a disempowered life as a girlfriend, wife, and mother, in a relationship with one partner for thirty years.

Prior to separating, for at least ten years — perhaps even more — I blamed my partner for my chronic discontentment and the despair of my unhappiness. The rising damp of resentment, hurt, disappointment, anger, and apathy accumulated and infiltrated my being. I had become the antithesis of who and what I imagined an empowered woman to be.

At fifty years old, I was barely breathing in a failed marriage, desperately lonely, scared for my future, and genuinely bewildered. How was I going to find the courage to overcome my deepest fear of becoming one of the fastest growing statistics of homelessness in Australia — the woman over fifty? Was my rise like a phoenix fantasy simply that — a fantasy — or was it possible to make the changes I needed to ensure the next chapters of my life were ones I could live authentically, joyfully, and of my own free will? If I could overcome fear and summon strength that had long ago been surrendered into helplessness, I could create a life where I was the empowered woman I yearned to be.

The Beginning of Empowered

Believing that the journey towards living the life I imagined would eventually deliver me to a prized destination of empowerment, I was delightfully caught unaware to discover I was wrong. Empowerment arrived not at the end, but with the decision to confront my circumstances with forgiveness for myself in my heart.

Over many weeks of sitting with this, slowly and gently, rays of light — the dawn of a new beginning — began to filter through the darkness. The awakening realisation that the feelings, emotions, and thought patterns I had conditioned myself to believe were "truth" had in fact contributed to my overwhelming loss of control was empowering. Attributing blame to my partner for the state of my marriage and the circumstances I found myself in was linked to the root of my disempowerment. Acknowledging this was empowering.

I no longer wished to surrender my time, energy, or power to negative thoughts or belief patterns that fuelled my despair, nor fight to change perceived injustices, nor attempt to have my version of events validated. This choice was empowering. I could not change my partner's behaviours or his version of the relationship's demise. Knowing and accepting this was empowering.

> *"He has a big part in the breakdown of this marriage. And he may*
> *never own that part. He may never apologise. He may never be able to*
> *understand or acknowledge your pain. But you played a role too.*
> *Even if it's only 10% of the problem — even if it's only 1%*
> *— you played some role in the relationship's demise.*
> *And that 1% is your path to freedom."*
> *— Sharon Pope 2016 p. 19*

What I could do and what I did do, was turn inward, focus on myself, and begin to stand in my power by accepting responsibility and accountability for my role in allowing years of resentment, hurt, disappointment, anger, and apathy to result in the neglect of self. In every situation, circumstance, or event that took me to that emotional and psychological place, I had a choice. I had a choice in how I responded and how I behaved. Often, I chose to enable behaviours that left me filled with disappointment, hurt, and anger. I rarely fought for my rights as a partner in the relationship. I did not stand up for myself, for my beliefs, or for any semblance of control over my life. I consistently took the path of least resistance to avoid the fight or argument I believed I could never win, nor negotiate a compromise in. Rather than fight the losing battle, I stepped aside

— and in doing so I chose to dwell, stranded in this harsh, unrelenting desert of hurt, anger, resentment, and disappointment.

Isolation and loneliness are disempowering. In my relationship I was isolated; there was no partnership, and I was desperately lonely. Throughout the relationship, the words "I love you" were rarely spoken. The absence of those words signalled from the beginning that unconditional love was unattainable. What I craved was friendship, companionship, and a confidante. Instead, I was bullied, controlled, and coerced. I did not defend myself. Why? The answer: lack of self-worth, lack of self-love, and no true understanding of who I was. I have very few "if only" thoughts, but in hindsight, if only I had known my worth and not 'settled' for just a handful of "I love you".

Women's empowerment has five components: a woman's sense of self-worth; her right to have and determine choices; her right to access opportunities and resources; her right to have power to control her own life, both within and outside the home; and her ability to influence the direction of social change to create a more just social and economic order, nationally and internationally.

European Institute for Gender Equality (2025)
https://eige.europa.eu/publications-resources/thesaurus/terms/1246

Accepting the part I played in my own journey into disempowerment was the first step on the journey to empowerment. I chose to no longer be a victim of a failed marriage to a domineering, coercive, and controlling partner. I chose to be a woman with the power to heal and change her life.

Finding the strength and courage to leave took two years of rebuilding my self-worth, self-love, and self-belief. I achieved this through a combination of yoga for physical and mental strength, energy shifting with a spiritual mentor for spiritual guidance, and the support of an incredibly talented psychologist to build emotional courage. To seek therapy and have my emotions and fears validated was a huge leap into empowerment. Therapy enabled me to salvage some self-respect on which I was able to build a foundation of self to start to plan my exit. I stayed in the marital home during this time and moved into my own room for the final eighteen months of the marriage.

Throughout this period, I was learning who I was, what my needs were, and discovering my authentic self. Learning to trust myself — and trust that I could create the life I wanted — were my greatest obstacles. Months passed, the pandemic came and waned. I persisted with physical exercise, continued to invest in my spirituality and understanding of self through yoga and energy shifting, and leaned heavily into the wisdom and lessons from my psychologist. Finally, understanding and believing that my destiny was entirely within my own control, I made the decision to leave — and set a date and time to do so.

Separation

I had very few friends and no close friends who were separated or divorced and this journey so far had been a very private one. It was virtually unknown in our social and even family circles what I was planning. I had no one to ask how to separate or opportunities to discuss and learn of other's experiences. In preparation, I drew strength and guidance from the book I Know It's Over... Now What? by Sharon Pope. This women's guide to preparing for divorce helped prevent paralysis from the fear of the unknown and gave me the tools I needed to have this unimaginably difficult conversation from a place of love, kindness, and respect — with gentleness and grace — not for my partner, but for myself.

"How you prepare for what will likely be one of the most difficult conversations of your life will set the stage for how everything unfolds from this moment forward. If you start with anger and blame, you will have a hurtful and uphill battle on your hands for many months, or even years. If you start with honesty and compassion, your chances of moving through this gently are much more likely."
— *Sharon Pope 2016 p.16*

When it was time to tell my partner that I was going to move out, I had no idea how he would react. There was never a guarantee that the approach I had decided on based on Sharon's book would diminish his anger, and I knew I could not control how he would treat me. But intuitively, kindness and compassion felt less like swimming against the current and more like moving forward in flow. Leading myself with self-love and dignity was a mirror for my partner. As a man I would describe as having poor emotional intelligence, limited communication skills, and a lack of empathy, this mirror offered him a framework to respond. Empowerment was delivering this news as the best version of myself — head held high with dignity; heart filled with grace — leaving him with little choice but to respond in kind.

The shift in power once I had delivered the words "I am not going to live with you anymore" was immediate. After the shock, his questions came hard and fast. What would that look like? What did it mean for our relationship? Would there still be a relationship? What did it mean for the five us as a family? Would we still be a family? Would we still work together? Would I still manage the business? What would be the financial settlement? I had the answers, and I delivered them calmly and kindly. For the first time I was empowered to say what I needed and wanted and I was heard.

I live with myself in the house of life

"For many women, to live alone is an empowering and deliberate choice. The solitude of living alone provides an opportunity to know yourself well and become comfortable in your own company. Women who choose to live alone can experience a greater sense of freedom, control and independence."
- Dr Catriona Davis-McCabe,
President of the Australian Psychological Society.

Living alone and describing myself as living "by myself" felt disempowering. Those phrases carried negative connotations of loneliness and failure. Instead, I chose to say: I live with myself.

"You can often change your circumstances
by changing your attitude."
- Eleanor Roosevelt

Empowerment has been learning to live with myself in the house of life — to know my worth, to make my own decisions, to surround myself with support, and to move forward with authenticity, freedom, free will, and the power to change. I quickly discovered that living with indifference in a relationship was lonelier than living with myself could ever be. I enjoy living with myself, and I have become very good at it. I am thriving, not surviving. Every day I am faced with opportunities to prove my self-sufficiency and capability. Society may perceive living with myself as synonymous with failure. My perception is that I am a champion — courageous, powerful, and resilient. Living with myself is an ongoing process of self-discovery and an opportunity for continual transformation. As I learn and grow, I rejoice that I am no longer required to remain the same to meet anyone else's expectations or demands. I am free and give myself the grace to be who I choose to be on any given day.

> *"Women who embrace solo living can discover happiness amid its numerous hardships, ultimately reflecting on their decisions with pride. It also offers women the choice to make decisions freely, nurturing self-reliance. This fosters personal growth and enhances self-confidence — traits women exhibit fiercely when empowered."*
> *— Ahmed 2024 para. 2.*

I have discovered it is infinitely better to be living with myself than be someone who wishes they were. Sometimes people suggest I am "lucky" to live on my own. It was not luck — the desire and will to overcome fear, to take the necessary steps forward, is what put me here. I have worked incredibly hard to make it a success. Living with myself is the most peaceful my life has been since my thirties. I once dreamt of a life like this during the times when my married life was miserable — and realising that dream has been deeply empowering.

On the rare occasion the feeling — or even the word — loneliness creeps in, I am able to recognise that it is my mindset, not the act of living alone, that shapes my perception. Learning to live with myself in the house of life has become my superpower. I am the curator of my own destiny with no compromise. I am strong, capable, sociable, and loving. I have much to offer personally and professionally — and this is not diminished by living with myself. I know who I want to be, and I have the freedom to be exactly that. Solitude is the prize of living with myself — those who do not have it often crave it. I do not underestimate the gifts of space and time — space and time to create my own future.

I am grateful for the privilege of living with myself — to do as I choose, and to take full responsibility for my life. This is not a privilege I take for granted. I am acutely aware of the suffering experienced by women whose circumstances are not as fortunate as mine — women who do not have the ability to realise a life like the one I have created.

Empowerment was finding the courage to choose freedom to live authentically as myself.

My empowering statements for living with myself in the house of life are:

- Empowerment begins at the precise moment a woman chooses herself.

- I love myself — that is why I live with myself, not because no one loves me.

- I am not what society assumes of a woman living alone — I am not a failure, and I am not lonely.

- I accept living with myself — not by myself — as a choice that brings me peace.

- As a woman who chose freedom and lives with herself and loves it — I am an inspiration to others.

About Jayne

At 58, **Jayne Hansford** is living proof that empowerment is not a destination, but a decision. After three decades in a marriage defined by coercive control, emotional isolation, and self-abandonment, she chose to dismantle the narratives that kept her small — and rebuilt her life from within.

Through two years of intentional growth — integrating yoga, spiritual mentorship, psychological support and deep self-reflection — she re-established self-worth, self-love and agency. Today, she lives with herself — not by herself — in the house of life she consciously created.

Her lived experience positions her as a voice for women navigating reinvention later in life, especially those overcoming disempowerment, fear-based identity, and the stigma of solo living. She speaks to the intersection of autonomy, identity, midlife reinvention, and the reclamation of personal power with authenticity and grounded lived truth.

Her message is simple and radical: solitude is not a sign of lack — it is a space for growth, clarity and the reclamation of self. She is not surviving. She is thriving. She is not alone. She is liberated. And she believes that empowerment begins at the precise moment a woman chooses herself.

@ jayneschulze5@gmail.com

ƒ jayneschulze

The Cultural Compass
Leading with Authenticity Across the World
By Elee Joven

"Your cultural background is your compass.
Navigate authentically and build bridges
where others see barriers."

My journey has taken me across 29 countries... and counting. From my birthplace on the tiny island of Guam, to the corporate boardrooms of the U.S.A. and ultimately, to building my own mission-driven speaking business. If I had to distill the greatest lesson I've learned about leadership - both leading others and leading myself - it is this: Cultural Intelligence (CQ) is the new currency of true influence. It is the foundation for resilience, the key to navigating ambiguity, and the superpower that allows you to thrive without compromising who you truly are.

Where I Am Now: The Bridge-Builder's Ascent

Today, I stand as a cultural intelligence speaker, mentor and advocate, committed to empowering immigrants, minorities and global citizens to transform cultural barriers into stepping stones. My ultimate vision is to create and inspire a cultural intelligence movement globally, positioning CQ as a "super skill for the future" and a household name.

How I arrived here is a story defined by both immense struggle and hard-won clarity. I am an "ideator" who enjoys discovering new ideas and different perspectives, and a self-described "resilient optimist". This resilience was forged early in life but did not fully embrace it until just two years ago.

I was born on the island of Guam in the 1970s, an American territory with less than 200,000 people. My grandparents raised me, and my grandmother instilled educational and business values in me, even if she insisted I become a doctor, attorney, or engineer - none of which I became. Instead, life threw me an immediate curveball: Just two weeks after graduating from high school, I discovered I was pregnant and became a young, single mother at the age of 18.

Although my pursuit of independence was derailed, it was not destroyed. I took on the responsibility, eventually married in 2000, and relocated to the US mainland just four months after getting married. The transition was not only challenging, but depressing, especially during the first two years. Coming from a Filipino heritage, pride can sometimes get in the way of communication. I did not discuss any of these challenges with anyone in my family - not my parents, kids, siblings, friends, or co-workers. Instead, I kept them all to myself.

Because that's what I knew.

That is the culture I grew up with - where open communication about life and challenges were not normal. And so, I toughened it out internally.

Life in the USA is constantly moving and fast-paced compared to island life. By then, I had four children and was the breadwinner in the family. Then in 2009, I decided to go back to university while still being employed full-time. A year later, I had to resign from my job so I could focus on my studies. My goal was to launch a shoe brand from what I learned, but instead, I faced profound instability after graduation in the summer of 2011 as this was the height of the GFC - global financial crisis. I quickly depleted my funds, with the ultimate blow resulting in my family and I being homeless, sleeping in a family friend's garage followed by cheap motels for four months.

The Invisible Barriers: Cultural Ignorance

In November of that same year, I was fortunate to return to the corporate world. I still remember my very first paycheck as it was used to pay for the first month's rent at a new apartment. New job, new place, new possibilities... I felt hopeful. However, despite providing technical and service excellence at work, my experience with organizational leadership was often defined by cultural blind spots. Multiple attempts at promotion in the organization where I worked were unsuccessful. Despite guidance offered on what I needed to change, the feedback was not landing effectively with me. Instead, some of the things I was feeling and thinking were:

"How did this person get the role when they don't even have a college degree?"

"I perform much better than this person."

"But I know more than this person."

"This person doesn't even know the difference between there, their, and they're."

"I get along with everybody, and yet, still not me."

"What do these others have that I don't?"

And my favorite - "I just won't and can't suck up to bosses."

The lesson learned here wasn't about the individual leaders who passed me over, but about the **systemic failure to recognize**

cultural intelligence on my part, and my perceived belief of my leaders' lack of, as well. These leaders, though perhaps well-intentioned and in my opinion, operated under cultural assumptions that penalized adaptation efforts. They failed to understand that my collaborative and relationship-building approach (often common in collectivistic cultures) was being interpreted as indecisive or lacking confidence in an American organizational culture.

Little did I know it at that time, but this period of constant rejection instilled a deep appreciation for resilience and authenticity. It taught me that cultural navigation is essential for turning survival into success. I realized that achieving success isn't just about personal grit; it's about building bridges to resources and opportunities across cultural divides.

The Future Lesson Learned: Working twice as hard wasn't enough if I didn't understand the "unwritten rules everyone else seems to know". My expertise was valuable, but often underrecognized because I had not mastered the cultural dynamics of the American workplace. **This painful professional setback became the catalyst for my deeper study of cultural intelligence frameworks**, which I only discovered when I went back to university (again) during the Covid pandemic.

Education in cultural intelligence became my lifeline.

My worst leadership came when I realized I led myself poorly for so many years by suppressing my authenticity while having too much pride to admit my shortcomings.

What exactly do I mean by this? To make a super long story short – I married someone from a different religion, and then converted to that religion thinking it was going to magically solve our many marriage problems... My gut was already telling me during Year 2 that I should separate. But instead, it was only after 12 years and "I-can't-take-it-anymore" frustrations of not being true to myself, that

I filed for divorce in 2013. For the first time in a very long time, I felt liberated that I could be myself again.

Lesson Learned: Ignoring my instincts in favor of external expectations led directly to emotional and physical breakdown. I learned the importance of setting boundaries and prioritizing my well-being. My current brand is now built on the power of authentic cultural navigation, a conscious rejection of suppressing my voice for assimilation.

The Turning Point:
Leading with Cultural Intelligence

However, the ultimate catalyst for redefining my leadership came during a period of loss. In 2020 during the pandemic, I lost my mother, brother and uncle all within three weeks. This triple loss created a deep recognition of time's value. I realized that time is our most precious and limited resource, and yet, I was spending it on others' expectations rather than my own purpose.

This awakening led me to resign from my corporate position in April 2022, despite the immediate depression and instability that followed. I knew I had to align my life with my core values: AUTHENTICITY, IMPACT, LEARNING, TIME CONSCIOUSNESS, and GRATITUDE.

The real breakthrough came when I combined my lived experience from Guam, the Philippines, and the USA, while also traveling across 29 countries and counting... I realized that my curiosity in diverse cultures and intuitive survival skills - reading people, adapting communication, observing differences, respecting these differences - could be systematized to help others.

My expertise isn't just theoretical; it's born from trial & error and necessity. I have lived the tension between effectiveness and authenticity. This led me to develop my proprietary C.R.O.S.S. Method™ (Connect, Recognize, Observe, Strategize, Shift) a framework that helps individuals find the third path: successful adaptation without sacrificing core identity.

Leading with the C.R.O.S.S. Method™ transformed my leadership from reactive assimilation to strategic autonomy.

- I transformed my underemployment struggle into professional expertise.

- I am building my speaking business - Elee Joven - focused on immigrants, minorities, and global citizens whom corporate training typically ignores. My approach prioritizes personal transformation through cultural intelligence over corporate metrics.

- I became a Pragmatic Visionary, balancing my future-focused goals with practical systems such as AI to save time (my focus on "time as currency").

- Ditching perfectionism. Personal development involves continuous learning and growth, and my mission is to empower millions with the same growth mindset.

- Success is defined by seeing my clients thrive when they move from one point to a much better point - not just financially, but in their personal, emotional, social and mental capacities.

A Leader Who Led Me Well:
The Power of Affirmation

The moment a leader validated my purpose and expertise being transformative happened in late 2024. I had the privilege of training with a speaking mentor from Australia - Sam Cawthorn. During a bootcamp in November, after giving a six-minute speech on cultural intelligence, Sam offered feedback: He said, I delivered the speech so beautifully, well-framed, and was "so close to being world-class".

As I write this today, I am actually pausing...

Again.

And again.

And again.

That feedback still gives me the chills, excitement and, believe it or not, fear.

Fear of the unknown, fear of failure, fear of making it, fear of being a global advocate, voice and face to cultural intelligence, fear of losing some part of me...

The fact that he said those words to me and didn't say it to anyone else in the room of approximately 35 students was a validation. When the day was over, he told me I was "way better" than a comparable speaker he'd seen just the previous week.

This experience taught me the profound impact a leader can have simply by affirming the unique gift and passion they see in another person. I realized my passion, not money, was the true motivator. This affirmation gave me the authority and confidence to embrace my mission as a disruptor.

Top 3 Tips to EmpowHer

My unique approach to leadership is rooted in balancing vulnerability with strategic action, authenticity with adaptability. These tips are derived from my methodology, designed to help women lead effectively while remaining truly themselves:

1. Embrace Cultural Authenticity as Your Superpower

Leadership starts with authentic self-awareness. Too often, professionals feel they must choose between being themselves and being successful. This is a false choice. Your cultural identity and background are assets that create unique perspectives for innovation and problem-solving. Connect deeply with your cultural identity foundations (the "C" in my C.R.O.S.S. Method™) and weave your authentic heritage into your identity (the "I" in my H.E.R.I.T.A.G.E. Method™). Lead from your core values, recognizing that integrity and transparency build deeper trust than perfect conformity.

2. Master the Invisible Rules - Decoding Cultural Intelligence

Technical excellence only gets us so far; leadership requires decoding the unspoken cultural expectations that determine perception. Instead of relying on rigid cultural maps, develop a "Cultural GPS™". This means learning how to Recognize cultural patterns and Strategize your approach before reacting (the "R" and "S" in C.R.O.S.S. Method™). When negotiating or leading teams, anticipate differences in communication style, time orientation ("time as currency"), and how feedback is given. Becoming culturally literate turns ambiguity into a strategic advantage.

3. Protect Your Time with Intentional Boundaries

Leadership is fundamentally about resource allocation, and time is our most precious resource. My personal journey through burnout taught me that urgent doesn't always mean important. You must be able to express and set boundaries, understanding that saying "no" can be perceived differently across cultures. Learn to balance cultural expectations with personal well-being. Focus your unique talents on high-impact activities while automating or delegating processes that drain your energy. Intentional choices about where you invest your time are the ultimate expression of leading yourself well.

My Enduring Vision

My mission is personal and deeply felt.

I am creating a world where cultural differences become bridges rather than barriers. I want to ensure that the "cultural intelligence revolution" benefits those who need it most - the underemployed immigrants, migrants, and minorities who are often held back by invisible cultural barriers despite their education and skills.

My legacy is the C.R.O.S.S. Method™ - a systematic pathway that allows individuals to maintain their authentic identity while successfully adapting across cultures. I want to be remembered for fostering a generation of cultural bridge-builders who carry forward this vision of connection and understanding.

My journey from being a teenage mother, the breadwinner for a family of six, experiencing homelessness, suffering from anxiety and depression (which was not even covered here) to a global professional proves that you can come from anywhere, overcome tremendous obstacles, and achieve your goals.

My struggle was the foundation for my expertise, and my commitment now is to ensure your path to leadership, life, and impact are clearer, more confident, and entirely authentic.

About Elee

Elee Joven is a Cultural Intelligence Speaker Advocate and AI Strategist committed to helping individuals embrace their cultural identity as a strength.

Born on the island of Guam and raised within a proud Filipino heritage, Elee became a single mother at 18, an experience that launched a journey of over 30 years in personal transformation. Having traveled through 29 countries (and counting), she brings a deep, lived understanding of culture's power to shape identity, resilience, and success.

Today, she empowers immigrants, migrants, minorities, and curious global citizens to discover their cultural superpower and thrive across cultures.

⊕ www.eleejoven.com

[in] elee-joven-745b2523

@ elee@eleejoven.com

The Courage to Be!! Me
by Josanne Falla

**A comfort zone is a beautiful place,
but nothing ever grows there**

'm a very ordinary woman who has lived a very fulfilled life.

Life and adventure and stepping outside my comfort zones are the very thrilling pieces that excite and terrify me at the same time.

The Beginning

I remember stepping outside our family home in a quiet leafy suburb on a warm and windy day in Melbourne in October 1988 with my husband. 2 children 8&3 with backpacks on our backs and one-way tickets across the world with excitement at the future and safety behind us.

We had resigned from work, sold our home and most things in it and were off on the adventure of a lifetime.

Just a few months earlier we were on a family holiday in Western Samoa when the chief of the village invited us into his Fale for cacao. He enquired as to whether we'd like to live there

And of course, this was tropical paradise, and we said yes, but what could we do for work. His answer unsettled us and changed our lives forever. Why do you need to work, he said, there's coconut in the trees and fish in the ocean.

Well, if you've been parents in Melbourne, with careers, and school runs and never enough time and always chasing the next dollar and wondering why, this was the call to action or the sign from above we needed.

We came home and the real estate agent was called the next day, and the new chapter of our lives began.

Naive, courageous, stupid, I'm not sure what you'd call us, but it was the best decision we ever made.

We had 3 months' worth of home schooling in our packs with drop off points for future long-distance education planned for Dan the 8-year-old. We kept it up for one week...

Month one was spent exploring the islands of Fiji, buying our fresh fruits and veggies from local markets, exploring the water's edge, climbing mountains and discovering local villages. The kids playing with locals, Ahn the taste of freedom.

We found ourselves on a tiny island living in grass huts, sleeping in hammocks eating fresh fish and drinking homemade pineapple rum.

Homework for Dan was writing about what he saw and learned? Books at night, spending pocket money at the markets, doing his own negotiations and the old 'times tables'.

From Fiji we moved onto Tonga, where the people were enormous and the lobsters came on a string of 8 for $10

I remember carting home a palm woven bag filled with crabs scrambling to get out on a crowded bus one day. Hilarious!

We moved on to Samoa straight into a cyclone. what an experience. so much water outside but none inside. The power and water were off for days. So, buckets of it were collected in the torrential rain to flush the toilets and wash the dishes. We went down to the harbour to see the boats upended and the trees covering the harbour. We bathed with the locals in a freshwater pool in our sarongs. We spent our first Christmas away, in the islands with minimal gifts under the broken off and decorated branch in our little home. A handheld fishing line and a handmade local doll for the kids.

They had no expectations, and we made frangipani leis and bought a delicious cake from neighbours and went fishing on the harbour ... the locals didn't celebrate Christmas at all, so we made our own. We flew over to Savaii and then on to American Samoa to explore further.

Next up were the Cook Islands where we managed to rent a house on the sand on the lagoon. We hired motor scooters and had the most marvellous time studying the lagoon and reef. Masks and snorkels were purchased- the kids learning to snorkel and I learned to scuba dive. The underwater world was mapped out, and science was taught the best way. Hands on!

We loved it there and made enquiries to buy a business and stay, however it would have meant boarding school in NZ for the kids if we were serious, and that was not what we were looking for .. plus there were many adventures still to come.

Our tickets and plan were to head to the states, get visas for central and South America and head to the end of the world. So now was not the time to set up house. We did delay our flights through, and luck was defiantly our side as the flight we were booked on crashed with most passengers dying. Of course we didn't know this at the time. News travelled slowly to the islands. One big lesson I learned there was that the locals shared everything and thought everything was to be shared.

Local kids had pinched our masks and snorkels, and the police explained this to us. We felt selfish and understood that perhaps their way was preferable to ours. We think that we bought them, so they belonged to us, whereas they thought the items were for everyone. I loved their way.

We never really own anything do we? It's all on loan, whether we pay or not.

The kids blossomed during our 5 months island hopping, we were all relaxed with sun bleached hair and tanned bodies, enjoying our days reading, cooking, meeting locals and ex pats and exploring the lagoons.

So, Los Angeles came as a bit of a shock, interrogations for hours at customs, driving on the other side of the road through spaghetti junctions, drug deals and stabbing on our doorstep. Of course we had to visit Disneyland, every child and adults dream, and we were staying in Anaheim the home of Disney. Yet the streets were not safe for our family and although we were warned that Mexico was very dangerous, we felt it had to be better than this and yes it was .... So much more welcoming and child friendly. The Mexicans welcomed us with open arms.

Our journey continued throughout Mexico on public transport. So many countries, so many stories, Brazil, Jamaica and then back through Florida where we bought a big American Cadillac, filled it with camping gear and headed through 26 states staying in national parks.

Onwards to Canada, over to England, Ireland, Europe and back home via Russia and Asia.

Two years of growth, education, exploration and learning.

Follow every rainbow – You don't have to see the whole staircase, just take the first step

We knew the warm air and the outdoor life was for us and we headed north to Noosa where we set up home for the next 35 years.

This was just the beginning of the becoming.

We bought a tiny business and the next chapter begins.

In the days, months and years that followed, my family and I grew.

I set up many businesses, some thrived, some fell in a heap

Laguna Signage Solutions was set up in 1991 when we arrived in Noosa and is still a thriving hub for businesses Australia wide today.

In those 33 years, I ventured into several other areas of business.

A business importing handmade jewellery from many countries (again trying to support women)

This was a home-based business where women could sell the gorgeous one offs to family and friends, giving them some extra income and was quite successful locally, in Victoria and in Europe.

Another super idea was the importation of reusable bamboo straws. I saw there was a horrific plastic usage causing enormous damage to our amazing environment and thought it was a fabulous product. Unfortunately, the cleaning of them to reuse was a bit tedious so didn't take off.

Another little side hustle was creating gorgeous wallpaper pictures to enhance decor, particularly useful in board rooms.

All the little ventures ultimately were not successful financially, yet the knowledge gained was immense.

All ideas need a lot of energy, commitment and passion to succeed. Determination and perseverance plus time.

I found that although my ideas are sound and come from the heart and that although enthusiasm is a wonderful instigator, attention to details, particularly when doing many things is vital.

Learning, Growth and Self Development- Change your thoughts and you change your world "Follow the whispers" not the loud voices

- Art is a passion of mine and allows me freedom to create without the need for finer details and I intend to pursue this creative outlet into my retirement.

- Having sold real estate when we first arrived in Noosa (the only job available) and as I really enjoyed my short stint in this area, quite successfully selling 6 properties in my first 6 months, I have continued to keep that particular interest alive by buying and selling residential, commercial and businesses over the years. Nothing ventured, nothing gained.

- During a course on self-development, I discovered ways to help myself to become a healthier, happier, stronger person and created an e self-help book which I called 28 days to happiness. Which encourages us to give ourselves a little bit of time every day just for ourselves. As busy working parents, we often neglect ourselves, but by prioritising ourselves for one hour a day, we can make massive changes. Yes, it does mean getting up an hour earlier but let me make this promise to you. Your whole life will change in just 28 days if you commit to this.

*During my self-development course I also learned that I needed to learn some new skills, one of which was public speaking.

So, I took up radio announcing on the local FM radio and absolutely loved talking to inspiring local women weekly on a show I called 'celebrating woman' over the next 4 years.

- I met so many incredible local women weekly that when I retired from the radio, I brought them all together to meet each other and my desire to create a lasting tribute to them was born.

- This book was created during Covid with two of the women I had met, a writer and a photographer and Women Inspired the book continues today.

- The desire to be around inspirational women was enormous for me and so I began inviting them to breakfasts, lunches and eventually retreats both overseas and then here in our beautiful Noosa to share their gifts and knowledge with each other.

**Surround yourself with people who inspire you to grow –
"Surround yourself with the dreamers and the doers, the
believers and thinkers, but most of all surround yourself
with those that see the greatness within you,
even when you don't see it yourself"**

The Noosa circle was created to connect, share, encourage and grow.

At one of our retreats in Noosa, our incoming Mayor Clare Stewart joined us to share her story and talked about some of the issues that were rife in Noosa, such as homelessness and Domestic Violence.

Covid had just begun to change all our lives forever; however, these were social issues that needed addressing now.

Clare encouraged me to bring the women we knew together to help feed the homeless. Which we did and raised an amazing sum of money.

Because we were raising money an NFP had to be established and WomenKind Australia Inc was created to stay transparent.

We went on to hold more lunches and the mayors' balls for the increasing need of support for women during COVID suffering DV and beyond to assist in helping in the housing crisis.

In this pivotal journey we have raised nearly $500k.

Looking inwards and growing outwards – *The unexamined life is not worth living*

Over the many years of my life, I have studied and learned many interesting things. I love to learn and gain knowledge to understand the world we live in.

I have learned about energy and healing through Chinese medicine and Reiki, I've studied accounting, lead lighting, Latin Dancing, yoga, meditation and qui gong. To name just a few. A master of short courses, an auto didactic, a seeker of wisdom.

*Luckily for me I have an understanding and supportive husband and partner of over 50 years who is very gracious when I'm off on my next adventure, whether it's travelling and exploring the world within with plant-based medicine, riding camels in the Sahara, hiking the Inca trail of Machu Picchu or walking solo from Portugal to Spain on the Camino,

I am naive and I've failed more times than I have succeeded however I've given it my best at the time and kept on trying.

I have learned to be real and authentic and just be myself.

I have been a people pleaser and wanted to be liked by everyone but learned that to like and love and to take care of myself is the only way to be real to myself.

A difficult lesson to learn, and still, I find myself offering my time and services to others, although less often than before.

My own feeling of peace is my current mission.
Am I a leader??
Yes - I lead myself boldly and bravely
But don't bother following me you might end up lost.

About Josanne

Josanne Falla is a passionate advocate for women's empowerment and a dedicated contributor to community wellbeing in Australia. Through her leadership with WomenKind Australia, she supports initiatives that provide women with crisis counselling, housing assistance, legal guidance, and financial support—ensuring that those facing hardship are met with dignity, connection, and hope.

Known for her strategic insight and unwavering compassion, Josanne brings a bold, purpose-driven energy to every project she touches. She believes deeply in the power of encouragement, collective strength, and the simple act of showing up for one another.

Josanne's work continues to uplift women across diverse backgrounds, creating spaces where they feel supported, valued, and inspired to rebuild and rise. Her commitment to positive change reflects her core belief: when women thrive, entire communities flourish.

@ Josanne.falla@bigpond.com

⊕ www.womenkind.com.au

Gentle Power

A Legacy, Lived

By Sneha Villalva

"Our daily words, actions and intentions
aren't just a mirror for us.
They serve as a compass for others to follow."

I count myself as wealthy beyond measure because I was given a rich inheritance from a long line of strong women. Gifts of generosity, grit, and grace. And taken all together, the grand gift of gentle power fueling greater purpose. These outlast anything material I could ever possess.

From my great-grandmothers to my grandmothers to my mother—every woman, a woman of steel and a woman of soul. Each dressed nobly—not in luxury brands—but wrapped in kindness, influence, resilience, and mercy, wearing their unique texture, pattern and color, much like the billowing saris they draped around themselves.

Annamma: The Gentle Power of Sacrifice

One of my great-grandmothers on my paternal side, Annamma, died when I was one year old, so I don't have any memories of her, just photographs. But those photographs hint at many stories never captured on film.

Annamma had flashing black eyes, an angular nose and a smile that mirrored the merriment and hint of mischief glinting in her face. I am told she would wisecrack with the best of them. She could put someone in their place so skillfully yet surreptitiously that they wouldn't recognize the scope of the reprimand until she was done.

Annamma was resourceful with the little she had, and cared for countless people in poverty even during times when she and her sons—my grandfather and his younger brother—were hungry themselves. She was a schoolteacher by training, living out a calling for ministry amidst great opposition. Her daily life was the greatest lesson she taught.

Annamma lived by the credo that it was better to give than to receive. She gave from a place of sacrifice, not abundance. Embedded in sacrificial giving is a belief that we are held to account for more than just how we and our family fare—we have a responsibility to both neighbors *and* strangers. Annamma could whip up a feast out of meager rations in record time and would feed anyone who came to her door. Undergirding that instinct was a belief that just perhaps she was entertaining angels unaware.

Gentle power acknowledges the inherent value and dignity of both the leader and the led. Leadership is grounded in respect, not rank. It is the big collective vision of rising *together,* interdependent and empowered; not the smaller individualistic dream of rising *alone,* independent and unencumbered.

Gentle power recognizes that we stand on the shoulders of giants who came before us, and that we advance when we are committed to mutual uplift rather than competition. Gentle power doesn't shed connection, it embraces it, recognizing that no one is too great and no one is too small.

Often it is those *under* the radar that will surprise us with their leadership.

Mary: The Gentle Power of Generosity

My late paternal grandmother Mary, who would one day be Annamma's daughter-in-law, was born in 1925 in India under colonial rule, in a society that had few options for women. But Mary defied patriarchy and cultural dictates for both gender and age.

At the age of 11, with her dark doe eyes gazing out over the crowds, she stood beside her father and other ministers and translated their sermons to hundreds—sometimes thousands—of listeners.

Theoretically, women weren't allowed to preach in those days. These were the 1930s after all. Yet it was my grandmother's schoolgirl voice that carried the message to people's hearts, long before the words *egalitarianism* or *feminism* were part of her culture's vernacular.

Also at a young age, Mary became the primary breadwinner for her family of origin.

Later, she oversaw more than 100 public schools in the city of Hyderabad, India, and later still taught both men and women at a seminary. Her authority was unquestionable because she led with unwavering belief.

Mary's core conviction was "radical generosity." It was tangible, not theoretical. She believed her God had been radically generous with her, so she in turn should not hold back from others. After caring for the needs of her family, she would give the rest of her money away to the poor. I never saw her turn anyone away. Mary's hands were always open, never clenched. Her heart was forever open as well. She befriended people from all beliefs and backgrounds.

Influence, which means the capacity to have an effect, comes from a Latin word—*influere*—which means to *flow* into. It's fluid. It moves *through*.

This understanding of influence runs counter to much of current culture and conventional wisdom. But it is true for the most effective leaders. Influence is *not* domination. It's an *invitation*—an invitation to pour in, not to squeeze out.

As former U.S. President Dwight D. Eisenhower famously said, "You don't lead by hitting people over the head—that's assault, not leadership."

Throughout her ninety-one years of life, my grandmother asserted her influence through pouring rather than pummelling.

Mary poured from a cup overflowing with inner strength, centered in her understanding that she was formed with intention, and confident that loving her neighbor put feet on her faith.

Pouring her presence, pouring out with conviction, and pouring in through service.

Presence.

Conviction.

Service.

That is what makes up gentle power—a triad of incomparable strength.

Most modern-day leaders may not embody this, but gentleness signals supreme self-control, without an iota of weakness. It is leadership with true influence and impact—it is leadership that outlives us. Strongmen are really straw men, and will inevitably fall. But a woman of gentle power is remembered, respected and emulated.

My grandmother Mary's lifelong display of gentle power through the generosity of her talent, time and treasure has left its mark upon me and serves as a consistent reminder.

I am especially reminded to exert gentle power through my words. I often tell myself that I can either create or destroy with my language. As a writer and speaker, I feel the sharp edge of this power daily. It is a sword that comes in many forms: my mouth, my pen, or my laptop keyboard. Like an expert swordswoman, we must wield our words wisely, judiciously, and strategically. We can say hard things. We must communicate difficult truths. But the *how* is just as important as the what. The words we use can build or break, heal or hurt. We can choose to either follow society, or lead it.

I believe our call in this age is to redefine cultural norms, reclaim our space, and return to the essence of influence. Annamma and Mary taught me well: **Gentle power is not only servant leadership. It is subversive leadership. It is leadership that unexpectedly turns tables, softens wills and changes minds.**

Laly: The Gentle Power of Perseverance

My mother, Laly, taught me another kind of subversive leadership. She displayed her power through her example of sheer grit.

Albert Schweitzer said, "Example is not the main thing in influencing others, it is the only thing."

We all know from our lived experience that true leadership begins in our immediate sphere of influence, the people who watch us day in and day out.

I would argue that no one—whether by their presence, their absence, their nurture or their neglect—is more immediately influential than mothers. The link between mother and child, even if separated, continues, because we know that children's cells actually live in their mothers' brains. The *December 4, 2012 issue of Scientific American*[1] has more on that.

My mom's intuition and instincts are so spot on I've felt like my mother lives in *my* brain.

That is actually more accurate than we might guess. A mother's example imprints us. Research shows that higher maternal resilience strongly correlates with higher resilience in daughters. Resilient daughters experience less depression and anxiety.

A mother's influence on her daughter's resilience is a kind of butterfly effect. Even a mother's tiniest act of courage or care when life is in chaos, shapes how daughters learn to deal with stress, endure pain, and keep a flame of hope burning when the cruelties of life try to snuff it out.

When my mother was diagnosed with breast cancer in 2018, she endured a brutal regimen of chemo and radiation. Her oncologist had never treated anyone as aggressively as she did my mother. Her surgeon later said she didn't know how to tell my mom how poor her prognosis was.

I watched helplessly as her body weakened from the treatment, uncertain which was worse, the disease or the cure. Food no longer had any flavor. Radiation scorched her body. Every ounce of her energy was depleted. It was considered a good day if she could stand up. Most days weren't good days. But in the midst of the medieval horrors of her treatment regimen, I witnessed a wonder.

My mom's physical strength waned, but her inner strength never dimmed. She often said she didn't fear death. That fearlessness is likely what gave her the courage to live. What she demonstrated to me day in and day out was a depth of tenderness and tenacity, gratitude and grit, I'd never seen before. My mother showed me what it was to be a warrior, to fight even when you're wounded.

That is leadership. That is gentle power. And that is an example I carry with me daily and will carry with me for the rest of my life.

We all carry those examples and we all bear the privilege of *being* examples ourselves. *Our daily words, actions and intentions aren't just a mirror for us. They serve as a compass for others to follow.* We leave only one set of instructions when we breathe our last. And that is the example we have set. It is not the main thing. It is the only thing.

As Marian Wright Edelman said, "You are the message that you send."

My mom's message was clear and resolute: Gentle power rises from perseverance.

Thankamma: The Gentle Power of Restraint

My mother's mother had breast cancer when I was in elementary school. She survived. It was finally cervical sarcoma that took Thankamma's life in 2006. What I remember of the years between was grace.

As the child of Indian immigrants in Southern California, I struggled with my difference. My schoolmates pointed it out on a daily basis. Cruel whispers in the classroom and taunts on the playground made me hypersensitive to anything that highlighted my un-belonging as a brown girl.

My grandmother Thankamma stayed with us at length twice, once when my second sister was born and again when my baby brother was born, each time for six months. She came to assist my mother, who was alone more often than not, since my father traveled nine to ten months of the year.

Thankamma was a bright light. She was tiny—I like to say, "fun-size"—but spunky. She had a full body laugh and she was always overflowing with concern, and would even defend me to my mother when I got into trouble.

But to my six-year-old eyes she also highlighted in sharp relief—sari-clad and with her halting English—that I was not white. As if my own skin did not betray me. I was embarrassed. And not a little. A lot.

I would run ahead of her on my way back from school instead of walking alongside her, keeping a distance that I thought would hide our kinship. Never mind that I was the only Indian at the time at Deer Canyon Elementary School.

But she never said a word. She was unfailingly gentle toward me.

Leading with restraint, rather than rebuke, requires an unusual depth of clarity about context and consequence.

Very likely my mistreatment hurt. Thankamma could have complained. Instead, she modeled power through grace. She knew who she was, knew who I was, and knew that time would teach me better than her tongue. Speaking up is important. But silence can sting more than sound. Many times it is louder, stronger—and higher. Former First Lady Michelle Obama encapsulated gentle power so well when she said at the Democratic National Convention, "When they go low, we go high."

The Gentle Power of Purpose

The high road of leadership is not an accidental route. It requires purpose and direction.

There are many times we feel like we are running in circles, chasing our own tails, unsure of why we are here.

Leading with purpose is not optional and it's not just intentional—it is *essential*.

Purpose means: the reason for which something is done or created, or for which something exists. If we don't lead with purpose, and don't have an intention and a goal, we aren't headed in any particular direction.

There were many times when I was a child when we would all climb in the big blue Plymouth family van and literally drive in circles around the neighborhood, looking at homes, or gazing at the skyline at sunset.

I treasured those times—but even those seemingly aimless moments were *intentional*: it was for the purpose of connection as a family, for recharging, and for renewal.

I recently read that in a race between a lion and a deer, many times the deer wins because the lion runs for food—and the deer runs for life.

Purpose is far more important than need. Seventy-four percent of Gen Z workers rank purpose at work as more important than a paycheck.[2] Purpose is our fuel, powering us through our best and worst days, carrying us through lonely and dark nights. It is what Simon Sinek calls our "why."

I am who I am because of the heritage passed on to me. Gentle power is a legacy lived—each of my foremothers swinging doors wide open in welcome, extending their hands to freely give, with their feet firmly grounded to endure, and hearts cracked wide open to forgive.

Gentle power is both inheritance and invitation. To step into the circle of those who have gone before and to welcome many more to come in.

Leaders aren't born. They are led.

1. https://www.scientificamerican.com/article/scientists-discover-childrens-cells-living-in-mothers-brain/#:~:text=In%20this%20new%20study%2C%20scientists,no%20evidence%20for%20neurological%20disease.

2. https://www.shrm.org/enterprise-solutions/insights/how-to-attract-gen-z-workers-with-purpose-driven-workplaces#:~:text=Gen%20Z%20employees%20crave%20career,a%20survey%20by%20Monster.com.

About Sneha

Sneha Villalva (*Snay-hah Vee-YALL-vuh*) is a speechwriter, storyteller, author and speaker.

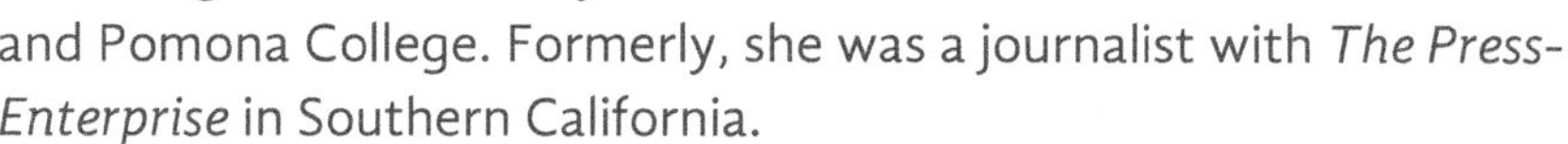

With more than two decades of professional writing experience, she served as the executive speechwriter for college and university leaders at UCLA and Pomona College. Formerly, she was a journalist with *The Press-Enterprise* in Southern California.

With a gift for blending strategic insight, empathy and narrative finesse, her work has appeared in National Public Radio (NPR), HuffPost, Associated Press, Sojourners, The London Reader, India Currents and more.

A Maxwell Leadership Certified speaker, coach and trainer and a member of the Speakers Institute Protégé cohort, Sneha has honed her craft among global thought leaders and top-tier communicators.

Sneha was named to MSN's list of Top 10 Leading Speakers to Follow in 2025.

Sneha's book, *Cut to the Essence*, will be released in May 2026.

Sneha is married to her first and last husband and makes her home in Los Angeles, California, USA, with extra dark chocolate always on hand.

🌐 www.snehav.com

@ sneha@snehav.com

in snehavillalva

The Show Must (Not) Go On
From Perfectionism to Possibility
by Jodi Gagné

"Happiness is not a checklist."

Today, my life feels different. There's now a softness I never knew. I've connected with an *aliveness* — an intimacy with myself and others, that has filled me in ways I never believed possible. Now, there is a deep understanding, kindness, and compassion for the *judged and criticized* parts of me that once believed they were never enough. My point of view is now acknowledged as *valid* and I honor what I feel, instead of overriding or negating it. I've leaned into the idea that there's no such thing as *right or wrong* experiences — only invitations to meet myself on a deeper level.

But it wasn't always this way.

I used to live a double life...what you saw on the outside was rarely a reflection of what was going on in the inside.

I protected myself with an armor of confidence and a sense of humor that was finely attuned to **'whatever you needed me to be'** because I couldn't take the risk of anyone looking too closely and seeing the cracks in my performance.

I struggled with my self-esteem and I saw every relationship as a transaction — if I was useful, I was valuable.

If I looked and acted like a *good girl*, followed the rules, got good grades, and got things done, no one would ask questions. They would simply assume that the *'keeping-my-shit-together'* façade was real and nothing was wrong. In fact, I created a version that was so convincing that it outsmarted detection — even from myself.

Skipping right through the crawling stage to walking, my drive for perfection and over-performing took root.

Then at the age of 10, we moved from Montreal to Toronto, and the innocence of my once simple childhood was shattered. I was bullied relentlessly, dumped by my best friends in elementary school and then again in high school, and later on in my twenties had a falling out with my mother-in-law, and a few other friends in university and beyond. What became very clear to me was that I was the common denominator, and I started to believe there must be something inherently wrong with me.

Busyness became my shield.

I am most believable when I am on stage, as told by my high school teacher 36 years ago, so the world became my stage.

At the age of 23, I was hit hard with the loss of friendships, a family health scare, multiple deaths in the family along with my father-in-law's cancer diagnosis and passing within two months, two miscarriages and a threat of divorce.

In 1999, while nursing my son, I began my studies as a wedding planner. 13 months later, I completed my exam for certification while giving birth to my daughter.

In 2001, the week of 9/11, I opened a business of my own. I built on my production and theatre experience and launched a wedding planning company which gave me an outlet for my creativity and flexibility to raise my family.

Regardless of what was happening in the world, I took my roles very seriously — nothing was going to slow me down — and my life became a series of checklists. The more I focused on what needed to be done, the less I had to feel the unsettling chaos in and around me.

Hustle became my normal.

Somewhere along the way, hustle became my normal and I became an expert at managing life's pressures — juggling the endless to-do lists and expectations until the constant hustle became my baseline. And because it was my normal, I didn't question it.

I knew the *show must go on* mentality better than anyone. And I was addicted to the adrenaline, pressure, deadlines — the high of pulling it off. And it satisfied my need to over perform and over deliver.

Quick share! As a lighting tech for a theme park's theatrical summer production, I pulled off a 44hr shift, only getting up to pee...my dedication and loyalty to the final product was intense! A badge of honor that I was very proud of at the time. **The final product was all that mattered and it didn't matter what it took to get there, as long as I got there.** It was all about the *finish line.*

As a wedding planner, it was all about planning for the future. I lived years ahead of myself. My mind was always on the next wedding — the one three weeks, six months, a year away. I was paid to orchestrate seamless perfection, to anticipate everything, control the uncontrollable, and deliver flawless joy.

And yet, through it all, no matter how many weddings and magical moments I created — I never felt good enough.

It took me over 15 years — and one unforgettable wedding day — to finally entertain the idea that I might have some talent. Ten minutes before my bride was about to walk down the aisle, an electrical fire broke out, leaving the reception venue condemned. While the couple were exchanging their vows, I was secretly finding a new location and replanning their entire reception, which I accomplished, in less than an hour — because the *show must go on.*

Looking back, I can see I was living in survival mode — overwhelmed, disconnected, numb.

But I couldn't see it then.

I have a theory: we might not be as okay as we think we are.

But the world is so damn noisy, how can we even tell?!

When depression hit me like a freight train in my mid-thirties, I spent most of my days in bed and railed against my own weakness, trying to "snap out of it." I was completely depressed, directionless, and burnt-out. I had nothing left. On the outside, however, it looked *simply perfect* (ironically the name of my wedding company) ...husband, kids, successful business, but inside — I was empty and numb.

I was consumed by guilt, shame, and frustration. I believed that I had no right to feel this way. I was overwhelmed by self-judgement and couldn't figure out how I could possibly 'fix' myself. I felt broken beyond repair and wondered if everyone would be better off without me.

It was around this time, I came across a quote by Eckhart Tolle:

"You are exactly where you need to be."

I sobbed. How could *this darkness, this* nothingness — possibly be where I needed to be?

I wish I could say that this moment cracked something open and that it was a turning point in my life. But it wasn't.

My doctor told me **not** to stop... to keep pushing through...so I did. And for the next decade it worked. I pushed harder, continued to cut myself off from my feelings, and showed up for everyone else while the cracks in my own foundation quietly widened.

I vowed that no matter what was happening internally, I would present the perfect image of control, and for the most part, I kept my depression, *my dirty little secret.*

Until recently, I didn't realize the cost. Somewhere along the way, I lost touch with myself. The busier I became, the deeper the ache was buried and the more numb and detached I became from myself and others.

It wasn't until I finally slowed down and looked 'below the surface' that I realized how not okay I was. The ache wasn't loud; it was quiet and constant, like a hum beneath everything. Once I finally stopped long enough to feel it, it was everywhere. And I couldn't fake "fine" anymore.

What I know now to be true is that reflection is one of our greatest untapped resources.

Taking the time to reflect wasn't a part of the first 48 years of my life. I lived in my head — efficient, logical, relentlessly productive. Feelings were messy, inefficient and a complete waste of time.

For most of my life, I saw emotions as something to keep in check. **I believed that to master my emotions, I had to sedate and control them.**

When the world shut down in 2020, so did my schedule — for the first time in 25+ years. I was forced to stop. And then a fog began to lift, a fog that I didn't even realize had been a constant part of my life. The sudden silence brought on a roller coaster of emotions — fear, anxiety, grief, anger — all at once. I began to get curious about who I really was without all of the distractions, labels, and obligations.

Silence can be deafening for the high-performer.

What I realized was I'd spent two decades living in the future, missing the very moments I was working so hard to perfect. My life was *fine* but it felt flat. I was craving something more, something deeper.

In 2021, I discovered the world of energy psychology and I pursued certifications in energy coaching and EFT (Emotional Freedom Techniques) also known as Tapping.

This thirst for a deeper understanding of the power of the mind-body-heart-soul was undeniable.

I became obsessed with needing to learn more. Not until recently did I discover that this need to understand was fueled by fear. The unquenchable thirst inside me *demanded* more courses, more training, and more certifications. Nothing was ever enough — until I acknowledged that I was looking to be fixed and I had unknowingly handed over this responsibility to everyone but me.

My pursuit for self-knowledge, my willingness to take responsibility, and my dedication to become more self-aware and conscious of my reactions is how **I slowly began to make the shift from performance to presence.**

And I owe a lot of credit to Tapping, a stress reduction technique — think acupuncture without the needles.

While I was training as an Energy Coach, I came across *The Tapping Solution* online. And out of curiosity, I tried a 16-minute Tapping meditation on "Not Enough."

What happened next shocked me.

Wave after wave of grief poured out — the kind that leaves you breathless, gutted, and yet somehow cleansed. It was as if the hurt I'd carried for years was finally acknowledged.

Within sixteen minutes, something shifted.

Tapping allowed me to begin to admit how not ok I was. It became the bridge between my head, heart, body, and soul — a practice that gently forced me to begin an honest conversation, to teach me how to be *with* myself, to deeply listen, trust, lead and support myself.

The performance filter through which I lived life began to fall away, and a rawness of presence began to move in.

During a weekend equine retreat in September of 2024, **I learned a lesson from a horse that took me even deeper into myself.**

When the horse turned, and walked away from me, I felt my heart being torn out. I remember feeling this intense pain of rejection. I could sense myself trying to reach out, trying to pull the life out of the horses, desperate for them to fill this void that felt so deep and painful. I felt an overwhelming sense of powerlessness, needing something or someone to fill it, because I couldn't do it for myself.

I realized that I was so focused 'out there' as opposed to 'in here' — chasing validation that I didn't realize that somewhere along the way I had traded self-loyalty for approval — trying to earn belonging. Each self-betrayal had led me further and further away from myself.

It turned out that I had more than one dirty little secret.

Until recently, I never connected any of my experiences to perfectionism. I used to think perfectionism was about having high standards or never making mistakes.

What I have come to learn is that it's way more subtle than that. It's the pressure to always be prepared. To hold it all together. Making sure nothing falls apart.

I was hyper-focused on 'being appropriate'', and not 'getting it wrong'. But in living like that, a stiffness sets in. Life becomes a checklist of right or wrong, and good or bad.

The real *aha* came when I realized **I was following invisible rules that I never questioned.**

Perfectionism, I understand now, isn't a flaw, it's a response. A way to shield ourselves from rejection, judgement and criticism.

But that shield? It's both a protection and a weapon. It numbs as much as it defends. And it silences the wild, intuitive parts that ache for more depth and aliveness.

It was the horse's rejection that helped me realize how freakin' empty I felt, the not-enoughness. It was a gut-punch. I saw it, I felt it. I could no longer keep the blinders on. I finally saw that in trying to protect myself from rejection, I was missing out on connection.

It is said that the longest journey you will ever take is 18 inches — from your head to your heart.

Energy work and Emotional Freedom Techniques help to shift out of autopilot. It helps you check in, before you check out. It's the interrupter — the pause between trigger and reaction. It gives the space to feel instead of fix. To get comfortable with being uncomfortable. And there is a relief when you acknowledge the 'suckiness' of a situation instead of trying to hide it or minimize it or pretend that you don't feel it or that it doesn't exist.

The more intentional and curious you become about your reactions, the more sensitive you become to the electrical *'zzzzt'* charge that courses through your body when you get *'hit'*.

In the beginning, because I was a master at minimizing and pushing through, I hardly felt the electrical zap. I soon came to realize that it was an incredibly tiny space between trigger and reaction — *that tiny space is a millisecond moment of calm where we can pivot the direction* — it's the window where we have access to choice.

I remember being completely floored every time I missed the window. I was actively working on this and yet, I would get hijacked so many times!!

And then finally, the practice paid off and I noticed I was more sensitive to the signals. I was aware of the subtle physical and emotional signs and followed the breadcrumbs of emotional clues — towards more ease, better decisions, increased productivity, compassion, and overall satisfaction.

What I've come to fully appreciate and honor is that **emotions aren't the enemy.** They're doorways into insight when you approach them with curiosity and compassion. Embracing this perspective isn't a one-time fix but an ongoing practice of responsibility.

My journey over the last few years has guided me to reclaim the parts of myself that I had kept hostage and reconnect with the woman I had unknowingly abandoned in my pursuit of perfection.

It's wild to think that my husband saw something in me that took me another 31 years to see in myself.

When you choose to stop running from what and how you feel, you make space for something extraordinary: truth, connection, and the kind of beauty and magic that shows up in ordinary moments.

Learn to see the breakdowns, breakthroughs, and the space between as sacred.

A friend once called them necessary dips. And they were right.

Don't skip the dip.

It's in the dip — the messy middle, the space between — where honesty awakens, connection expands and growth lives.

Life is paradoxical. It's messy and beautiful, heartbreaking and hilarious. It's not either / or. **It's both / and.**

When we can hold all of it without needing to fix or escape, we open the door to something deeper. No matter what may be happening around us.

As a recovering perfectionist and lifelong seeker of control and approval, I continue to honor this journey of self-knowledge — the more I learn, the less I know. I continue to let go of the need to make sense of everything or have it all figured out.

Because in the end, all of this — the softening, the reflection, the courage to feel — is an invitation to move from a place of centeredness rather than woundedness.

It's taken years to understand that happiness isn't something to check off a list. It's an inside job. True joy lives in the freedom to be who we are — to create, to express, to feel fully alive.

That means no longer sacrificing joy for the pursuit of perfection — but choosing, again and again, to be present, to meet life as it is, and remain open to receive it all.

My Empowerment Tips

1- Get curious, not critical.

Instead of judging your emotions, see them as information. Every feeling offers insight — a clue to what's really happening beneath the surface. Lean into the power to feel, not just fix.

2- Find your interrupter.

Cut through the noise and pause the autopilot. Notice the space before reaction — it's where your access to choice lies and your response becomes intentional.

3- Don't skip the dip.

Honor the messy middle. The space between breakdown and breakthrough is where honesty awakens, connection deepens, and trust anchors.

About Jodi

After 30+ years in the fast-paced world of theatre, weddings, and events, **Jodi Gagné** knows what it's like to run on caffeine, perfectionism, and the 'show must go on' mentality. She built a career out of making things look effortless — even when it wasn't.

With a Bachelor of Fine Arts from York University in Toronto, Jodi went on to build Simply Perfect, a wedding management company she led for more than 22 years. When the pandemic brought everything to a halt, she was forced to see how disconnected she felt from herself and life. That pause became an invitation to reconnect with the woman she had unknowingly abandoned in her pursuit of perfection.

Now, an Energy and EFT Practitioner and founder of In Flow Energy Coaching, Jodi supports high-achieving women who've spent years hiding behind a mask of success — externally accomplished yet internally unfulfilled, disconnected, and drained. For women running on empty, tired of checking all the boxes, and ready to step into 'not this anymore' — where 'I'm fine' is no longer cutting it. Together, they uncover what's buried beneath the busyness so they can restore a felt sense of aliveness and become their own source of meaning, motivation, and fulfillment.

🌐 InflowEnergyCoaching.com

📷 Inflowenergycoaching

ⓕ inflowenergy

19

From Ashes to Wings
What I Had to Release to Rise
By Ashley Levin

**"You rise the moment you release the stories
that keep you small."**

There are dates you forget, and then there are dates the whole world remembers. March 19, 2020. California was shutting down. Governor Newsom had just declared a two-week stay-at-home order, which, looking back, is comical, and I was standing on my lawn with my neighbor around seven in the evening, listening to the announcement through her car radio like we were in some kind of low-budget pandemic movie. Except it was real life.

But here is what mattered more than the shutdown. How I felt leading up to it. I was not just unhappy. I was drowning on dry land. I was going to therapy. I had been doing the work for years. I was talking, analyzing, unpacking, and none of it was actually shifting anything inside me. I still felt not good enough.

I had even picked up a prescription for an antidepressant, already playing out the fantasy. I would take the pill and suddenly I would become Jasmine and "A Whole New World" would start playing in the background. But my body said absolutely not. Not because medication is wrong. It is not. But because my body was done. Done carrying all this pain around. Done expecting something external to fix an internal problem.

Something in me snapped. Quietly. Softly. But decisively. I did not want to cope. I wanted to change. I did not want to survive my life. I wanted to rise inside it.

So on that lawn, with the world shutting down and my inner world begging for something new, I turned to my neighbor and said, without thinking, planning, or understanding why, "I am coming out of this better than I am going in."

It was not motivation. It was not empowerment. It was not even confidence. It was a declaration. A decision. A line in the sand between the woman I had been and the woman I was finally ready to become. And that single sentence became the match that sparked my fire. I did not know it then, but that was the moment my rise began.

Seeing the Stories

In the weeks after that day, I began noticing the stories I was telling myself. Not with fireworks and a big reveal, but with the slow uncomfortable awareness that comes from seeing something you cannot unsee. It would happen in the smallest moments. Someone took an hour too long to text back and my mind instantly began to spiral, filling in the blanks. They hate me. They are done with me. A plan would change and somehow it meant something about me. It was almost impressive how quickly I could turn nothing into something.

What struck me was not just the speed of the stories but the certainty behind them. My brain did not say, maybe she is upset. It said, "She is". It did not suggest, perhaps this means I am not important. It declared it as fact. I realized I had been living inside these narratives for so long that they felt like truth. Automatic, familiar, and strangely comfortable.

These stories did not begin in adulthood. They were old. They were familiar because I had carried versions of them since childhood, long before I had the language to challenge them. They were the quiet beliefs I had learned to build a life around without ever questioning if they were mine.

The more I paid attention, the more I saw it. The reflexive interpretations. The way I filled silence with fear. The way I assumed the worst before anything had even happened. It became glaringly obvious that I was not reacting to life itself. I was reacting to the version of life I had created in my head.

And this noticing was the first moment something inside me softened, a quiet unraveling of a story that had shaped me for years.

Facing What I Had Been Avoiding

Seeing my stories was one thing. Facing them was another. It required looking into a mirror I had spent most of my life avoiding. A mirror that reflected not just my patterns but the parts of myself I had learned to hide, dismiss, or explain away. It was uncomfortable. Humbling. Sometimes painful. But it was honest. And for the first time, I realized it was the doorway to everything I wanted.

As I sat with these parts, I began to understand something I had never considered before. Every story I told myself existed because on some level it had served me. Not necessarily in a healthy way. Not in a way that expanded me. But in a way that felt familiar enough to become a kind of emotional shelter. Even the painful stories had benefits. Even the limiting beliefs had logic. Even the narratives that hurt me were protecting a part of me that did not know how to feel safe without them.

Once I understood that, something softened. It became easier to accept these pieces of myself. To see them not as flaws or failures but as old strategies. Outdated, yes, but once necessary. And acceptance, I learned, is what makes change possible. Because you cannot release what you are still fighting. You cannot rewrite a story you keep trying to outrun.

When I finally saw the benefits I had been getting, the certainty, the predictability, the emotional protection, the illusion of control, I realized I did not want those benefits anymore. I wanted different outcomes. Different relationships. Different versions of myself. And that meant I needed different stories. Stories that supported the woman I was becoming, not the girl I had been.

But the release was not just mental. It was not as simple as telling myself a new thought or choosing a new belief. My body had been carrying these stories for years. Sometimes decades. They had shaped my reactions, my posture, the tension in my chest, the tightness in my voice. So, letting them go meant learning to let go physically too. To unclench. To soften. To breathe in a way I had not breathed in a long time. It was the most intimate kind of undoing. A slow unwinding of old meanings. A gentle returning to myself. And it marked the beginning of a different life, not because everything suddenly changed, but because I did.

Shifting the Way I Saw Everything

From that point on, the way I moved through my life began to shift. Moments that once sent me spiraling now felt like invitations to choose differently. Conversations felt clearer. Decisions felt easier. And for the first time, I was not responding from old wounds. I was responding from an emerging version of myself.

The first real change was not dramatic. There was no breakthrough. What shifted first was simply the way I saw things. And I know how cliché this sounds, but it really did feel like taking off glasses I did not know I was wearing. Everything around me started to look different, even the way my reactions showed up.

Instead of jumping straight into old conclusions, the worst-case scenarios, the self-blame, the reflex that said this must mean something about me, I started to notice what was happening before the spiral. I caught the moment where a story tried to form. I caught the meaning I wanted to assign. And for the first time, I had enough awareness to pause and wonder, is that actually true or is that just familiar?

That tiny pause changed everything. I became more curious, more open, more willing to observe instead of assuming. The old patterns did not disappear, but they stopped feeling automatic. And once they stopped feeling automatic, they stopped feeling like truth.

It was strange at first, almost disorienting, because I had spent my whole life believing my reactions were who I was. But suddenly I could see the space between what was happening and what I thought it meant. And in that space, I started choosing differently. Not perfectly. Not every time. But enough to feel a shift. And that shift felt like relief. Like breathing room. Like I was not bracing for emotional impact every five minutes.

Seeing differently did not solve everything, but it changed the way I moved through my life. It made me feel more present, more grounded, more awake to myself. And once I could see myself clearly, I could not go back to the version of me who was living inside every old story as if it were fact.

Finding Truth Instead of Positivity

One thing that became clear during this process was how different it felt from what I had been taught for years. In therapy, the message was simple. Identify the negative thought and replace it with a positive one. But no matter how many times I repeated the new thought, nothing inside me shifted. The old story still felt real. The new one felt like something I was trying to talk myself into. It was not because I was resistant or unhealed. It was because the new story was not true.

That was the part no one explains. You cannot build a new story on top of a lie. You cannot take a narrative rooted in fear and try to plaster something positive over it and expect your mind or body to believe it. Eventually you stop trusting the process, and worse, you start to think you are the problem. But the problem was never me. The problem was the method. I did not need a positive story. I needed a true one.

That is when something clicked in a way it never had before. I needed an honest one. A believable one. A story that felt solid enough that I could actually stand on it. So instead of trying to invent a version of myself I did not recognize yet, I started looking for the parts of my old story that were not fully true. Not to deny my experience. To separate the facts from the fear. And once I saw the difference, the new story was not something I had to force. It was not something I had to convince myself of. It was something that emerged naturally, almost quietly, from the truth that had been underneath the whole time.

And that truth, not positivity, not pretending, not wishful thinking, was what finally gave me something real to rise from.

Integrating the New Truth

Once I started telling myself stories that were actually true, something in my life began to change. Quietly. Almost imperceptibly at first. I did not wake up one morning as a new woman. There was no dramatic transformation, no cinematic breakthrough, no 'Whole New World' score playing in the background. What shifted were the smallest moments, the ones I had never paid attention to before.

A text would come in with a tone that normally would have sent me spiraling, and instead of collapsing into the old meaning, I would pause. I would breathe. I would give myself enough space to ask the question that had become my anchor. What else could this mean? Sometimes the answer came easily. Sometimes it did not. But the pause itself was proof that something inside me was rearranging.

Little by little, I started choosing interpretations that did not hurt me. Not out of denial, not because I was trying to be positive, but because the old stories no longer felt like the only option. I found myself responding from clarity instead of fear. From groundedness instead of panic. From truth instead of habit. And the more I did it, the more natural it became.

This was the integration. Not perfection. Not certainty. Repetition. Repetition that slowly rewired the way I moved through the world. Repetition that built evidence for my new identity. Repetition that showed me I did not have to live inside the old version of myself anymore. It was not about being a different woman overnight. It was about becoming a different woman one moment at a time.

The rise was not loud. It was not dramatic. It was steady. And that steadiness was the first time I felt like enough.

Rising With What Life Brings

As I continued choosing stories that were true, not familiar, my life started rising with me. Opportunities began showing up in ways I could not explain. People entered my life who reflected the woman I was becoming instead of the woman I had been. Doors opened that I did not know were there. The things I used to chase began arriving without force. And the life I thought I had to earn slowly became the life I could simply choose.

My business grew from this place. Not from strategies or pressure or hustle, but from alignment. From telling myself the truth. From choosing differently. From becoming the woman who no longer needed to live inside old stories to feel safe. The more I trusted myself, the more the world trusted me. The more I rose, the more my work rose with me. The more honest I became, the more my purpose unfolded.

And somewhere in that unfolding, something became clear. What I had walked myself through was not just a personal transformation. It was a process. A pattern. A path. And over time it became the framework I now guide other women through. Not as theory. As truth. As lived experience. As the steps I took to rise from my own ashes into the woman who could finally spread her wings to fly.

And that is how I ended up here. Writing this chapter. Receiving an invitation I once would have never believed was meant for me. Everything I am living today is the direct result of one choice. The choice to stop believing the story that kept me small.

None of this happened by accident. It happened because I stopped believing the stories that kept me small. Because I returned to the woman I was never allowed to be. Because I built a life on truth instead of fear. This is not the ending of my rise. It is the evidence of it.

Here I am today, writing these words, living this life, receiving this opportunity, because the moment I chose a truer story, my entire world had no choice but to change with me.

When I look at my life now, the opportunities, the alignment, the way things unfold with a kind of ease I never knew before, I can trace all of it back to one thing. Not the moment life changed, but the moment I did. The moment I began shedding everything that was not true, everything that was not mine, everything that kept me small. Because that was the moment my rise began. That was the moment my wings finally had room to expand.

Taking the First Steps to Rise

1. Ask yourself, what story am I telling, and is it 100 percent true?

Every spiral begins with a story, not the situation itself. Gently name the story you are telling, meet it with compassion, and then ask the question that interrupts the pattern: Is this fully true?

2. Identify what in the story is not true.

Look at the actual facts. There is always an assumption, fear, or meaning you added that does not hold true. Naming what is not true softens the emotional charge and reveals your actual truth.

3. Choose the truest version you can believe today and practice it.

A new belief becomes real through repetition. Each time you choose the truer interpretation, you teach your mind and body a new pathway to rise.

Standing in the Truth of My Rise

I am so grateful for the choice I made on that lawn that night. I think of the version of me who was still trying to outrun her stories, who believed she had to earn her worth, who had no idea she was allowed to rise. And then I look at my life now, the work I do, the women I walk beside, and I know the truth. A woman's transformation begins the moment she finally stops gripping her old stories and lets them fall to ash. What rises from those ashes is not a new version of her, but the truest one, the one who had been waiting beneath the layers all along. My rise taught me how to lead myself, and that became the foundation for how I now lead others.

Your wings do not appear when life gets easier.
They appear when you finally stop carrying
what was never yours to hold.

About Ashley

Ashley Levin is a trauma therapist turned feminine empowerment mentor who has spent twenty years studying the emotional blueprints that shape people's lives. As a therapist, clinical supervisor, and private practice owner, she worked with hundreds of clients and became known for facilitating deep emotional transformation. She is trained in Ketamine-Assisted Psychotherapy and Internal Family Systems and created The Whole-Body Trauma Healing Workshop, a CEU-accredited training for therapists, that established her as an innovator in trauma-informed care.

Today, Ashley stands at the forefront of feminine empowerment as the founder of In Her Power, where she guides women through her framework From Ashes to Wings, a transformational process drawn from her own lived experience and her two decades of clinical mastery. Her work blends emotional clarity, identity expansion, and feminine leadership to help women release the stories that once kept them small and rise into the women they were meant to be.

Ashley is also the creator of the upcoming podcast *In Her Journey: The Patterns That Shaped Us and the Rise into Our Power*, which explores the emotional and energetic architecture of women's lives. She is currently building a global movement rooted in truth, self-trust, and embodied power.

🌐 InHerPowerment.com

📷 inherpowerment

Shift and Lift
You Can't Lift Performance Until You Shift Communication
by Tracy Tully

"Motivation is where a woman's resilience begins. It sparks courage, builds confidence, and powers her leadership journey."

It was February 2011; I found myself in the middle of a rising flood. As a school principal, I was expected to attend school during floods until they were closed, so I was travelling to work in a boat. Along the way, I made desperate phone calls to the Director General of the Queensland Department of Education, requesting permission to close the two schools I was managing to protect the safety of students and staff. Three times I rang; three times my requests were refused. Their decision was made with no regard for human safety, driven by political considerations. I chose to defy their order, closing both schools.

Following departmental policy, I reported the director general's failure to approve my repeated requests to close the two schools, a potentially catastrophic breach of human safety and well-being, during an emergency. This was the person at the highest level of leadership, responsible for the ultimate protection of the state's public-school students and staff. The professional and personal hardships experienced by staff during this flood were entirely preventable, and the dire consequences of that leader's refusal to close the schools prevented staff from returning home to protect their families and save their possessions. Every staff member was affected, with their safety at risk, and several staff members lost significant personal belongings, including family photos, furniture, and vehicles.

My actions had extreme and appalling consequences for myself and my family, in the form of a hideous 'political payback'. I experienced the full force of the department's wrath backed by a corrupt government. I became a whistleblower, punished with the intent to 'keep me quiet' and to protect the senior leaders involved. At the time, I had no idea I was an expendable pawn in a high-powered, party-political game of government chess, intricately woven into the lead-up to the state elections. I was informed that it was believed I could single-handedly sway votes in my electorate. Inadvertently, I had unlocked a well-hidden door, exposing mind-blowing corruption and fraud at a level I could never have imagined.

I authored a book, sharing my journey to help others who found themselves in the same position, and there were plenty across all occupations. Inspired by Theodore Roosevelt's *Man in the Arena*, I penned a heroic prose, 'She Rises From the Fire', Page iii, published in my first non-fiction book, *'FEARless Buckle Up ... Build RESILIENCE'*, Tracy Tully (2019). It was while creating the fifth paragraph that I recognised who I was ... *"She is the one who stands strong in turbulence, who struggles unaided, making mistakes; who bravely travels alone. ... For she fears less and dares to challenge them all.'*

FEARless is dedicated to those *"whose power of speech inspires others by courageously giving voice to the voiceless, for a more equitable future world."* (2019) Page iv. I use my book to speak about building resilience in the face of fear and have become sought after by corporate organisations, not-for-profit companies, print media, radio, and national TV for my thoughts and opinions. As a media personality, I use the strength of my influential voice and expertise to speak out on behalf of those who cannot and are too afraid to do so. Educational employees across the nation are bound by a code of conduct that prohibits them from speaking out publicly without their employer's approval — and that is never granted. As an independent expert with a 38-year career in education, I can connect with educators and listen to their stories and concerns. With my career knowledge and powerful voice, I have spoken candidly at international and national events about building resilience in the face of fear.

During this turbulent period of my life, it took years to understand who I'd been and where I am now in my leadership journey. Deep inside, I was struggling with my identity, and I don't mean pronouns! There was something I couldn't explain happening to me ... until I finally recognised it was grief for a life not lived. Facing the daunting prospect of what happens when the identity I built as a school principal no longer fits.

I became someone new; all those years I thought were lost were spent rebuilding the foundation of my being, and I didn't recognise it happening. The shackles that bound me as a political pawn of my past disappeared. What emerged was confidence and clarity about where I was heading in my new world, and I decided to rebrand myself.

Shift & Lift Australia emerged as I focused on my occupational expertise, knowledge, and passion for speaking and writing. I recognised that the prominent obstacles hindering all management conversations and decision-making were often due to poor-quality leadership communication and a lack of active listening. Improve on these areas, and visibility expands.

The Rise of Conversational Leadership

You Can't Lift Performance Until You Shift Communication.

Shift & Lift Australia © SHIFT & LIFT Australia

www.shiftandlift.com.au

At **Shift & Lift**, we empower leaders and teams to rise above the noise - to be seen, heard, and remembered.

My mission is to help people present themselves more effectively in every conversation and enhance their perception in every room. Assisting to lift their performance or shift on.

I assist others by elevating their Profile, strengthening their Presence, and increasing their Poise by mastering two key aspects: raising their visibility through effective use of their voice.

When you communicate with clarity, courage, and connection, VISIBILITY becomes your global influence. It's not about speaking louder; it's about talking with purpose, power, and impact.

Shift & Lift – The FOUR MODELS

MODEL 1: The SHIFT Model – From Fear to Influence. SHIFT how you show up – LIFT how you're seen.

MODEL 2: The LIFT Model – Visibility in Motion. Visibility is a cycle, not a moment.

MODEL 3: The 3P Model – Profile, Presence, and Pause. When you LIFT your voice, everything rises – your Profile, Presence, and Poise.

MODEL 4: The VOICE Model – How Visibility is Built. Your VOICE is your vehicle for visibility.

The Rise of Conversational Leadership – The Silent Cost of Poor Communication

"The communication crisis is costing Australian Businesses Millions."
Tracy Tully

Poor communication is silently eroding the productivity, engagement, and profits of Australian workplaces. From mismanaged meetings to avoided conversations, organisations are losing billions of dollars on wasted time, burnout, and talent turnover. As a Leadership Solutions Specialist, I am on a mission to shift how we speak and lift how we lead.

In the era of automation, conversation has become the human advantage. I credit future leadership belonging to those who communicate with heart, not hierarchy. With a career in education spanning four decades, I understand why education in Australia has declined so rapidly over the last thirty years. There's a lack of meaningful and critical dialogue in our schools and educational workplaces.

We find ourselves in the era of Conversational Leadership, a modern leadership philosophy that focuses on the power of meaningful dialogue to shape culture, inspire trust, and drive organisational performance.

It is the practice of using conversation rather than commands to influence, align, and engage people toward shared goals. Rather than relying on hierarchical directives, Conversational Leaders foster open, authentic communication that encourages participation, curiosity, and collaboration.

Conversational Leadership is critical when dealing with difficult people.

"Winning an argument is a losing game. Winning means that you've lost something far more valuable – their trust, their respect, or worse, the connection. The only reward you've won is their contempt."
("The Next Conversation Quotes by Jefferson Fisher - Goodreads")

At its core, Conversational Leadership means leading through connection, not control. It involves:

1. Active listening to understand, not respond.

2. Creating psychological safety so people feel heard and valued.

3. Encouraging curiosity and inquiry to explore diverse perspectives.

4. Using questions to guide discovery, reflection, and innovation.

5. Building relationships that turn information exchange into shared understanding and action.

Conversational Leadership: Know your personality.

I always knew I was an ADHD personality, and as a school principal, I certainly didn't require a WISC test to prove it! I spent a lifetime without the benefit of the simple, science-backed systems for working with, rather than against, a procrastinator's brain – designed around motivation, reward, and momentum. Today, I understand the mindset of a procrastinator. It is a stress and dopamine regulation issue, and through years of research, I have come to realise how it affects our work performance, communication, and relationships. With this understanding, I can better support myself and others through my business consultancy.

In an education career starved of prominent leaders, two leaders stood out: Regional Directors Bob McHugh and Dr Stephen Brown, both of whom shone like beacons on the horizon, serving as inspirational leaders and mentors. Bob taught me the importance of clarity and consistency in communication, and Steve influenced me with the courage and discipline of structured and informed 'Critical Dialogue' - embracing quality feedback through active listening and summoning the courage to be curious about what could be.

> *"Only those who will risk going too far can possibly*
> *find out how far one can go."*
> *"T. S. Eliot - Only those who will risk going too far can..."*

On a personal and private level, my parents were intrinsically my strongest leaders, and their impact on my lifelong learning was monumental. Holding me close yet pushing me far to discover how much I could expand. Upon their passing, my sisters picked up the baton; my 'wing women,' shifting my dependence on merely travelling on the motorway to taking off from the tarmac; lifting my wings so I could fly again.

As a senior school principal, Leadership was given 'lip service' and that's where it started and ended. Singularly, the leader who failed me the most was the director general, who refused my requests to shut down two schools in an emergency situation during a monumental flood. However, that decision saved more lives than we'll ever know, as it resulted in a new statewide school policy granting school principals the power to make the decisions for their schools, rather than relying on public servants in the head office with little knowledge of the local worksite, geography and conditions.

I am courageous enough to admit my own leadership failures, and in my 38-year career in education, as others before me, I have had many. Given the state's lack of leadership and management at the time, it was challenging to make decisions due to limited knowledge and outdated attitudes. On reflection, there were several areas I can highlight, including: not being a member of a particular political party; a lack of time-relevant communication when it was necessary for understanding; the scarcity of information when I didn't have it;

and a deficiency of empathy when I was too exhausted and time-poor. All share a common feature: a lack of effective Conversational Leadership. This is where I found *Critical Dialogue* to be my most valuable and insightful friend. Embracing this strategic tool repeatedly enabled me to stand on the balcony and look down at what was happening around the nation; that bird's-eye view, which we too often forget during turbulent times. In television media, this is a crucial skill, along with the ability to write and speak with courage, while confident that my disruptive words are fact-checked with cogent evidence from 'those in the firing line,' living the experiences daily.

It was the training and reflection in Critical Dialogue that led me to understand the communication deficits I experienced while working with others, guiding me down the path towards Conversational Leadership. The potent power of clarity and consistency in communication cannot be overstated; I have consistently pursued this approach in my business.

It is in Conversational Leadership that I have found my passion and achieved business success. A vast majority of people struggle with basic communication skills, and it's no fault of their own, as they haven't received adequate training in communication, either during their formative school years, post-school study or in the workplace. Conversational Leadership is a powerful and practical skill; building that expertise in our work teams is critical to business growth and sustainability in this fast-paced world of commerce.

In business and leadership, we must continually upgrade our personal and professional development, just as vehicles require regular maintenance. All leaders have a duty to share their knowledge, skills, and expertise with those on their teams. I had the honour of travelling to Italy to participate in and speak at the Leading Ladies Lunches LLL Retreat hosted in Tuscany by Amir Makhlouf and Catherine Molloy. Catherine presented her communication sessions, and in one of them, she discussed the importance of understanding our personalities. This is an area of great interest to me, and the impact was both rewarding and significant, both personally and professionally. The takeaway for me was to gain a deeper understanding of myself, and I left with the resolve to get to know myself by delving into my past and reflecting on how I have developed, which led to writing this co-authored chapter.

If you have the curiosity and courage to explore and reflect on your past, to unlock the secrets of change opportunities that are hiding in plain sight but invisible to you, then I encourage you to write. Become a member of the Leading Ladies Lunches LLL global Leadership network, and watch your wings expand, your view of business widens, and the horizon that was once limited magnifies tenfold. You will travel to places you never thought possible, with the strength of friendship and the power of networking, resulting in exciting collaboration opportunities.

Join here: www.leadingladieslunches.com

- Don't underestimate your influence.

- Don't downplay your impact.

- Never forget — your words can become another's inner voice.

The question is: What kind of voice do you want echoing in their head when the world tells them they're not enough?

"Be the voice that reminds others they are capable, worthy, and standing before a future rich with possibility. You are the author of belief, the one who lifts limitations, and the difference-maker who shapes outcomes. Every single day, you are given that opportunity - use it with purpose." Tracy Tully

Top Tips to EmpowHer

Active Listening for Transformational Communication

1.Asking Open-Ended Questions

Tips:

- Use 'what', 'how' or 'tell me about'
- Keep questions curious
- Allow silence for thinking

Traps:

- Avoid 'why' questions
- Don't hijack the conversation
- Too many questions overwhelm

2. Avoiding Interruptions and Judgements

Tips:

- Let silence encourage deeper sharing.
- Show empathy with posture.
- Pause before responding.

Traps:

- Giving advice too early.
- Finishing their sentences.
- Showing impatience.

3. Paraphrasing or Summarising

Tips:

- Reframe what you heard in simple terms.
- Keep paraphrasing neutral.
- End with a check-in.

Traps:

- Twisting their meaning.
- Over-explaining.
- Paraphrasing too often.

In Summary

Conversational Leadership is not about talking more; it's about talking better.

It shifts leadership from issuing orders to inspiring ownership, and lifts tolerance from controlling outcomes to co-creating them.

Businesses that adopt this approach foster cultures where effective communication becomes a competitive advantage, enhancing engagement, innovation, and overall performance.

About Tracy

Tracy Tully is a powerful voice reshaping conversations that matter. She has appeared across major media, including Channel Nine's A Current Affair, The TODAY SHOW & TODAY EXTRA, Channel 7's SUNRISE, Channel 10, SKY NEWS, ABC, and on Russell Brand's podcast, influencing critical debates with courage and clarity.

A professional speaker, TV/media personality, and author, Tracy is known as a percolator of resilience and a distiller of fear. As a Leadership Solutions Specialist at SHIFT & LIFT Australia, she champions The Rise of Conversational Leadership — because, as she says, "You can't LIFT performance until you SHIFT communication." She equips leaders and teams with practical tools in conversational communication, influence, confidence, and strategic thinking.

With almost four decades in education, Tracy swapped her school whistle to become a whistleblower, sharing her story in FEARless Buckle Up ... Build RESILIENCE. She is also a co-author in multiple leadership and women's anthologies and founder of East2West Publishing, helping authors share brave, unfiltered stories. Her children's book, Gordon the Goat and the Gully Kids (2026), brings Australian adventures to life for the next generation.

🌐 www.shiftandliftau.com

in tracy-tully-3879a2122

@ shiftandliftau@gmail.com

The Fire That Shaped Me

A Journey of Embodied Leadership, Self-Trust, and Returning Home to Myself

by Dr. Mini Kaur Rattu

"A woman becomes unshakeable the moment she stops abandoning herself."

I did not become a leader because someone handed me a title. I became a leader the moment I stopped betraying my own inner knowing.

For most of my life, I thought leadership meant endurance—an endless capacity to hold, to fix, to rise above. As a Punjabi Sikh woman raised between cultures, I grew up with an unspoken curriculum of strength: *be grateful, keep going, don't complain.*

I wore that strength like armor. It made me high-achieving, ambitious, resilient—and also quietly hurting, disconnected from my body, and unable to recognize when I needed support myself.

What I did not yet understand was that leadership isn't the performance of strength. It is the integration of strength and truth.

My truth took decades to name.

This is the story of how I found it, lost it, reclaimed it, and learned to lead—not from survival, but from embodiment.

Where I Am Now:
A Life Built From the Inside Out

Today, I am a Licensed Clinical Psychologist, a Yoga Therapist, core faculty at Stanford Psychiatry's YogaX program, and the creator of mind-body frameworks used by high-performers, clinicians, and healing professionals nationwide. I teach nervous-system science, trauma-informed leadership, and embodied resilience. I speak on stages. I lead retreats. I work with executives, athletes, physicians, and leaders who want to regulate their inner world so they can rise in their outer world.

But my authority does not come from credentials.
It comes from lived experience—
from surviving trauma,
from healing in layers,
from breaking patterns that were never mine to keep,
and from choosing myself over and over again, even when it terrified me.

The world sees the polished version now. Very few saw the versions of me that were still trying to belong, trying to prove, trying not to break.

This chapter is that story.

The beginning:
A Childhood of Silence and Strength

I was born in Daly City, California, raised by immigrant parents who carried their own histories of generational trauma, migration, resilience, and sacrifice. In many Punjabi families, emotions are not the language of love—responsibility is. We show we care by showing up, by working hard, by surviving what must be survived.

I learned early that I was expected to be the strong one:
the reliable daughter,
the high achiever,
the one who didn't make trouble,
the one who understood without needing anything herself.

But beneath that outward competence, my nervous system was a storm. I grew up with unspoken emotional wounds, cultural pressures, and relational ruptures that shaped how I saw myself. I would later learn the clinical terms—attachment wounds, emotional deprivation schema, subjugation schema, self-sacrifice schema. But back then, all I knew was that my needs felt too heavy for others, so I learned to bury them.

When you silence your needs long enough, you begin to disappear from yourself. That became the root of my trauma—and the beginning of my leadership story.

The Trauma that Changed Everything

In my mid-twenties, I entered a relationship that would alter the trajectory of my life. I loved deeply, but the relationship quietly eroded pieces of me—my confidence, my intuition, my sense of safety. It was emotionally abusive in ways I didn't yet have the vocabulary for. I internalized every rupture as my failure.

When my arranged marriage ended, I felt like I had shattered. I didn't just lose a partner—I lost the version of myself I had built around that relationship and how I believed others perceived me.

For months, I spiraled in shame and grief. I hid the truth from everyone, including myself. I still remember sitting on the floor of my apartment in complete silence, unable to feel anything except the weight of my own self-blame.

But breakdowns have a strange way of becoming openings.

That moment—though devastating—forced the beginning of my awakening.

It taught me the difference between strength as endurance and strength as self-honoring.

It taught me that ignoring your pain is not resilience; healing it is.

And it taught me that leadership begins the moment you decide to walk toward yourself rather than away.

The Mentor Who Led Me Well: My First Glimpse of Empowered Leadership

During this period of rupture, I worked under a supervisor who changed the course of my professional identity. She didn't empower me through grand gestures—she empowered me through presence, attunement, and embodied leadership.

She led with:

- **Clarity without harshness**

- **Compassion without over-functioning**

- **Confidence without ego**

- **True mentorship—holding space while still challenging me**

When I doubted myself, she reflected back what she saw: *competence, intelligence, potential.*

When I abandoned myself, she reminded me gently: Trust your voice. It is stronger than you think.

She modeled what I had never seen in my personal life: a woman in her power who didn't need to dominate or diminish anyone to lead.

This was my first experience of **regulating leadership**—leadership rooted in nervous system stability, relational attunement, and emotional safety.

It left an imprint that would later shape the leader I became.

The Leader Who Disempowered Me: What Happens When Leadership Lacks Self-Awareness

A few years later, I encountered the opposite—a leader who operated from fear, insecurity, and ego. Someone who used shame instead of guidance, urgency instead of clarity, and pressure instead of presence.

Under this leader, I learned:

- Confusion is a sign of poor communication, not poor competence.

- Shame is not a motivational tool—it is a nervous-system dysregulator.

- A leader's emotional instability becomes the emotional climate everyone else works in.

- Disempowerment is not a reflection of your worth—it is a reflection of their unhealed wounds.

That experience taught me a truth I use with every client, student, and leader I work with now:

You can learn from leaders who empower you—but you often learn even more from the ones who don't.

From her, I learned how not to lead:
I learned to never weaponize authority.
I learned to never neglect humanity in pursuit of performance.
And I learned that leadership built on insecurity collapses quickly.

Leading Poorly:
The Season My Strength Became a Shield

I am not proud of every leadership chapter in my story.

There was a period early in my career when I led from over-functioning. I was the stereotypical high-achieving woman therapist—hyper-competent, over-prepared, emotionally available to everyone but myself.

I said yes when I was exhausted.
I held others when I was hurting.
I led with resilience but not regulation.

Because I had not yet healed my trauma, I led from the part of me that believed: *If I don't show up perfectly, I will be abandoned.*

This made me a strong leader, but not always a sustainable one.

One day, after months of burnout, I realized that my leadership had become a performance. I was delivering excellence at the cost of my own well-being.

I had to ask myself the question that changed everything:

"If you stripped away obligation, fear, and cultural conditioning—who are you truly trying to become?"

The answer required me to soften.
To heal.

To dismantle my survival identity.
To rebuild not from pressure—but from truth.

This was the turning point of my leadership.

When I Led Well:
The Birth of My Embodied Leadership Framework

The first time I knew I was leading from the right place was during the creation of my program UNSTUCK: Burnout to Breakthrough. It combined psychology, polyvagal theory, and yoga-based somatic practices—everything I had learned, survived, and embodied.

Instead of leading from perfectionism, I led from *purpose.*
Instead of managing others' nervous systems, I regulated my own.
Instead of hiding my story, I shared it.

The impact was immediate:

- Clients felt seen, not judged.

- High achievers softened long-held armor.

- Leaders reconnected with their bodies and intuition.

- Burned-out professionals found new pathways toward sustainable success.

I saw, in real time, what empowered leadership does—it liberates others to rise.

It was the first moment I knew I was doing exactly what I was born to do.

My Healing:
Returning to My Body, My Culture, and Myself

As I deepened my own healing, I began revisiting parts of myself I had long abandoned.

I reclaimed my Punjabi Sikh identity—not as a point of difference but as a point of spiritual inheritance. The resilience of my ancestors lives in my blood. Their survival, their migration, their grit—it exists in my Annamaya Kosha, the physical body I inhabit today.

I reclaimed yoga not as a Western wellness practice, but as its original philosophy: **a map for remembering the Self.**

I healed relational patterns that once kept me small.
I learned to recognize safety in my body.
I learned to regulate my nervous system instead of performing resilience.

And slowly, I returned to myself.

This is what empowered leadership actually is:
 Not power over others—
 but power within yourself.

The Woman I Became:
Leading With Integrity, Embodiment, and Truth

Today, my leadership is rooted in three core principles:

1. **Embodiment** — I cannot lead others somewhere I haven't gone myself.

2. **Integrity** — My outer leadership must match my inner alignment.

3. **Service** — Leadership is not image; it is impact.

I lead with warmth, boundaries, cultural humility, trauma awareness, and science.

I lead from the body.

I lead from truth.

I lead from the belief that empowered women empower entire generations.

I am no longer the woman who needed to be chosen.

I am the woman who chooses herself—and teaches others to do the same.

The Three Best Empowerment & Leadership Tips for Women

1. Your nervous system is your leadership superpower.

Regulation is charisma.
Presence is influence.
Safety is strategy.

A woman who is grounded in her body cannot be manipulated, minimized, or dismissed easily.

2. Do not lead from the wound—lead from the wisdom.

Your trauma may inform your empathy and intuition, but healing transforms those qualities into power rather than patterns. When you lead from wisdom, you guide with clarity instead of reactivity.

3. Never abandon yourself—not for love, not for leadership, not for belonging.

Every time you silence your intuition, you reinforce self-doubt. Every time you honor it, you strengthen your inner authority.

Self-trust is the foundation of empowered womanhood.

Closing:
The Woman Who Returned to Herself

If my life has taught me anything, it is this:

Your story does not make you broken—it makes you whole.
Your wounds do not weaken you—they widen your capacity.
Your healing is not a detour—it is your becoming.

I was born in Daly City, California.
I now live in San Diego, California.

But spiritually, emotionally, and as a leader—
I live in a place I built myself.

A place of self-trust.
A place of regulated strength.
A place where my identity is not something to negotiate, but
something to embody.

And if there is one message I want every woman who reads this to
walk away with, it is this:

You are allowed to lead your life on your own terms.
And the moment you choose yourself—fully, fiercely,
unapologetically - you become unstoppable.

About Mini

Dr. Manmeet "Mini" Rattu, Psy.D., M.S., is a Licensed Clinical Psychologist, internationally qualified Yoga Therapist, and speaker whose work bridges neuroscience, psychology, and yoga-based somatic healing. Based in San Diego, she specializes in the neuroscience of stress, trauma, anxiety, and high-performance wellbeing. Through her integrative approach—rooted in cognitive-behavioral therapy, polyvagal theory, and trauma-informed yoga—she helps individuals move from chronic stress and survival mode into clarity, resilience, and embodied confidence.

Dr. Rattu serves as core faculty with Stanford Psychiatry's YogaX Program, where she teaches mind-body courses and developed a pioneering module on Ancestral and Collective Trauma. In her private practice and national workshops, she provides actionable, science-backed tools for nervous system regulation, emotional mastery, and sustainable mental health.

A competitive NPC bodybuilder and wellness educator, she also speaks on the intersection of mental health, movement, nutrition, and resilience, advocating for a holistic and culturally attuned model of self-care.

Her work is dedicated to helping high achievers, leaders, and healing professionals cultivate regulated presence, inner strength, and lives aligned with their deepest truth.

🌐 drmini.com

@ info@drmini.com

📷 dr.mini_kaur

Accidental Hero
by Catherine Molloy

"It's not merely the power you're given;
it's the path you choose that
defines your impact."

The plane plummeted without warning, and the screams were deafening. Outside my window, the wing wobbled like a thin piece of cooked spaghetti flapping in the wind. Time seemed to stretch; every second felt like an eternity. Across the aisle, Jennifer's face was pale, her mouth open in a scream. I caught her eye and mouthed one word: "Pray. "I looked around at the rows of beautiful Saudi women. Why scream when we could pray? In their culture, they had been taught to turn to prayer in times of crisis.

"Pray out loud," I urged. And so, we did—together, our prayers rising *Inshallah* above the chaos.

We survived, as you can tell. But those seconds felt like a lifetime.

It was 2016, and we had left either Dubai or Doha—I can't quite recall now – en-route to a remote city, Sakaka, in Saudi Arabia. I later learned that on that same day, forty people were being publicly beheaded in Chop Chop Square in the capital city, Riyadh. It's no wonder the air felt heavy with tension- as if even the sky itself was rebelling.

It's remarkable how, in moments of turbulence, whether in the air or in life, everything slows down. Clarity emerges in the chaos, and you instinctively you know what needs to be done. Have you ever been in a moment of danger when time seemed to freeze, and suddenly the path forward became crystal clear?

Sometimes in life, when we can't change a situation, the only thing we *can* change is how we see it. For me, faith has always been a guiding light. I believe deeply in the power of collective prayer— when voices unite, hearts align, and we seek the same outcome together. You see, praying is still an action, so in every crisis, if I can't solve it or find someone who can, I still take action - through faith.

Looking back, I realize there have been many moments when I've become my own accidental hero - simply by finding strength in faith, believing I can, and taking the courage to act. And I'm certain that, when you reflect, you'll find in your own way, you've been your accidental hero too.

The Bank and the Bully

I'll never forget being sixteen. My mum had died suddenly, and I took a job at the bank. To make things easier, they transferred me closer to home. But life was then made harder by a colleague — let's call him Glenn. He was two years older, with a bright orange tuft of hair and a habit of lying through his teeth. Our job was to batch and balance the days cheques and payments. Whenever something went wrong, he blamed me; when it went right, he took the credit.

The seniors in the office must have thought I was truly hopeless until rostered days off were introduced. This meant we worked a little longer each day but had a day off a month. So, when Glenn was rostered off, everything balanced perfectly—because he wasn't there to help me. When I was off it was chaos—because he had to do the work. I quietly went to the accountant and asked him to take note of what was occurring.

Glenn soon was transferred (a promotion, of course), and on his farewell day, he told me how much he liked me and asked me out. Well, let me tell you—that was never going to happen. Back in the day, this was just cruel manipulation; what he did today, you would call it *gaslighting*!

So, he left, and we slickered (balanced first time) every day on time without a problem. A confidant said he would get caught out one day, and sure enough, at this new branch, within two months, he was asked to resign. The truth had finally caught up with him. I can't remember, in my fifteen years in the bank, anyone ever being asked to resign.

How did he get away with this for so long at our branch? How was I criticised for over ten months, crying each day going to work to have to face ridicule and deceit? The manager soon approached me and apologised to me for what I'd been through under my so-called supervisor Glenn. I became a bit of a hero in the branch - balancing faster than ever before. What would have happened if I'd resigned? What if id given up?

Heroes aren't born in moments of glory but in the quiet decisions to keep going.

I believed in myself and my skills. I knew what was happening, and I had faith that the truth would surface. It did- through time, a simple roster system that exposed the truth and me speaking up. I stumbled into courage one choice at a time and found the hero I never knew lived within me.

I soon went on to top sales monthly – first in the branch, then statewide, and then nationally. Without that noose around my neck, I could fly. Did it create resilience? Absolutely. Determination?

Without a doubt. It also left me with a lingering drive to always prove myself — to work harder, do better. But now, I remind myself: *I am enough*. And so is the next person.

When I reflect today, he wasn't a bad person. His intention was that he wanted to look good, and for that to happen, he had to make someone else look bad. The new branch did not fall for this, and he was called out. Maybe, just maybe, if he had a growth mindset, he may have learnt the skills, so he was not always making mistakes. Maybe there could have been a better job role for him. Obviously, figures and balancing were not his strong point.

So, he was my not-so-great leader who accidentally taught me the importance of training others, being nice, and helping others when they are struggling. You see, bad leaders teach us what not to do, and great leaders show what's possible. He accidentally taught me what is totally unacceptable in business, and this has stood me in good stead.

Bad leaders teach us lessons that good leaders never could.

Lessons in Leadership

An absolute hero of mine was Mr. Steele, my Year 9 English teacher. We would debate sentences, words, and meanings and he gave me a love of English and for learning. My Grade 1 teacher, Mrs. Partridge, sparked my lifelong love for education. My mum – my greatest role model - adopted me, loved me deeply, and built her own thriving pottery business that grew large, and bought her own car. I loved her entrepreneurial spirit—you would call it that today. I loved my father's incredible mind and kindness for all living things.

I was soon transferred and promoted a few times and ended up in the commercial centre dealing with the million plus clients and preparing the legal documents for the bank.

I have always liked to get things right—cross the T's and dot the I's. One manager stood out to me, a big tough guy, with a huge heart for helping customers achieve their dreams.

Unfortunately, on my return from overseas, before I headed back to the office, I was filling my car with petrol—and so was my boss. I was excited to see him. A great leader energises you, engages you, empowers you. I called out, "See you Monday!" He shook his head. "No, you won't." I called out the client's name; he said, "Yes."

He backed the wrong client, and the loss was too great for the bank. He was put on the chopping block. His replacement a loud prideful man with no empathy, no growth mindset, and no respect for the team culture. Once again, I found myself under a" leader" *but not a leader*.

This time I asked for a transfer. I protected myself from destructive leadership. That was growth. From my best leader, I learnt rules exist for a reason, and you need to follow the rules when they are someone else's you are working for. If you don't like their rules, and they don't align with your values get out and find a culture that does align.

You see, the mistake my great leader made was overstepping the guidelines for people he liked. I have now learnt rules are in place for a reason, and if they need to be challenged, then go through the correct procedures and don't just change them yourself. Life is a learning journey.

Today I run a volunteer leadership program worldwide. Some of the stories in this book are from our leaders around the world. Once a month, our leaders from around the globe give their time to build leadership skills and serve their communities. You can also join in for free—by going to www.leadingladieslunches.com and finding a lunch in a time zone that you would like to attend.

When you look back on life, when have you stood up and been your own hero? What's your story?

My Empowerment Framework

The Hero's Toolkit to Cultivate Your Inner Strengths

H: Harness Self-Awareness

Understand your strengths, weaknesses, and emotional triggers. Keep a journal to reflect on your actions and reactions in various situations. Knowing yourself is the first step toward making heroic decisions.

E: Embrace Challenges

Embrace challenges as opportunities to grow. Regularly put yourself in situations that test your comfort zone—whether it's speaking up in meetings, volunteering for difficult tasks, or tackling personal fears. Resilience is built on tackling one challenge at a time.

R: Respond with Intent

Practice pausing before reacting. In the heat of the moment, take a breath and say out loud, "What's the best action I can take right now?" This intentionality helps you respond rather than react impulsively.

O: Optimize Mindset

Develop a growth mindset. View setbacks as learning experiences and focus on solutions rather than problems. Use positive affirmations and visualize successful outcomes to stay mentally strong.

Harnessing self-awareness means truly understanding who you are—your strengths, weaknesses, emotions, and how you respond to different situations. It's about taking the time to reflect on your actions, recognize your patterns, and acknowledge what drives you. When you harness self-awareness, you become more mindful of how you show up in the world, allowing you to make better decisions, improve your relationships, and respond more effectively in moments of stress or challenge. It's like shining a light on your inner self so that you can navigate life with clarity, confidence, and authenticity. This self-awareness becomes a powerful tool, guiding you to act intentionally rather than just reacting to whatever comes your way.

Embracing challenges means facing difficulties head-on rather than avoiding or fearing them. It's about seeing obstacles not as barriers but as opportunities to learn, grow, and strengthen yourself. When you embrace challenges, you step out of your comfort zone, take on new experiences, and push your limits, knowing that each challenge is a chance to improve and evolve. It's like training a muscle—the more you work through challenges, the stronger and more resilient you become. Embracing challenges is saying "yes" to growth, even when it's tough, and trusting that you have what it takes to overcome whatever comes your way.

Respond with intent means responding to situations thoughtfully rather than impulsively. It's about taking a moment to pause, assess, and choose your actions deliberately, instead of just reacting out of habit, fear, or emotion. When you respond with positive intent, you're in control—you're aligning your actions with your values and goals, ensuring that what you do or say reflects who you truly are and what you want to achieve. It's the difference between being driven by the moment and consciously driving the moment yourself. By reacting with intent, you make decisions that are purposeful, impactful, and often lead to better outcomes, both for yourself and those around you.

Optimizing your mindset means actively shaping the way you think to support your success and well-being. It's about cultivating a positive, growth-focused attitude that helps you see possibilities instead of obstacles. When you optimize your mindset, you're training yourself to focus on solutions rather than problems, learning from setbacks, ` and staying motivated even when things get tough. It involves replacing negative self-talk with empowering thoughts and staying open to new ideas and perspectives. By doing this, you create a mental environment that encourages resilience, creativity, and continuous improvement, making you more adaptable and ready to handle whatever life throws at you.

Learning new skills, building resources and tools and then putting them into practise has been what has helped empower me too.

A Moment That Changed Everything

At a recent training session, a lady embodied exactly the **H.E.R.O** framework. I had planned to discuss something entirely different, but instead, I introduced the concept of decisions being "heavy" or "light." Before I step on stage, I always set the intention that the right words will come at the right time for the right people. This was one of those moments.

I encouraged the audience to make decisions not just with their head or heart but to really listen to their gut—because sometimes, our intuition knows the way, even when we're unsure. What feels heavy? What feels light?

After, the session, when everyone left or so I thought, a woman approached me and said, "Catherine, I want to let you know something. Tomorrow, I'm scheduled to have an abortion. But the more I think about it, the more I realize I couldn't live with myself afterward."

I want to be clear to you, the readers—I would never tell anyone what decision to make in a situation like this. It's deeply personal, and there is no right or wrong answer from me, as it is each individual's situation and life. But when she told me that the decision felt so heavy, that she knew she couldn't bear it, it was clear this moment was altering the course of her life. She decided to keep her baby, and eight months later, she sent me a photo of her beautiful little baby boy.

What she didn't know was that she was speaking to me—someone who had been adopted, and then lost both adoptive parents, with my mum passing when I was just sixteen. Her choice resonated deeply with me, and it highlighted the power of trusting your own inner voice.

I've seen the other side too—a dear friend of mine was taken for an abortion by her mother when she was sixteen, and she never truly recovered from the emotional weight of that decision.

Decisions like these are monumental, and it's crucial to make them for yourself, free from outside pressure. If you can't see yourself moving forward with a choice, that's your gut speaking to you.

On that day, this woman became her own accidental hero by making the choice that felt right for her. She found joy and peace in choosing the lighter path (it may not of been the easier path)—but it aligned with her deepest instincts. That day, she listened to herself, and she was her own hero—she saved herself and her baby.

Being your own hero is making the choice that is right for you.

But if someone has made a decision for you that doesn't resonate with you, let it go now. Don't carry the weight of it—let it go. Don't be weighed down by the past. They did what they thought was the best for you at that time.

Learning from it is how we empower ourselves.

My Empowerment Tips

- **Listen to your gut and follow it** — Does it feel right? Does it feel light?

- **Know how to energise yourself instantly** — Smile, say something positive, adjust your posture — find your spark.

- **Use the HERO Framework** — Harness, embrace, respond, and optimise.

- **Have faith** — You can be the hero you want to see in the world.

So, if you're reading this and a decision is weighing on your mind — pause. Ask yourself:

Does it feel heavy? If so, don't do it ...reassess... Does it feel light? Great... Does it feel right? Do it ...

Trust that your gut will guide you toward your light — the choice that's right for you.

Sometimes, simply listening to that inner whisper is all it takes to become your own accidental hero.

By falling, I learned to fly.
By breaking, I learned to build.
And by accident, I learned — we can all be our own heroes.

About Catherine

Catherine Molloy is an award-winning international speaker, author, and communication expert with over 25 years of experience transforming the way people lead and connect. As the founder of **Leading Ladies Lunches Global Online,** she champions conscious leadership and creates opportunities for women worldwide to collaborate, grow, and create meaningful impact.

Renowned for her *HERO* framework — Human behaviour, Engagement, Relationships, and Outcomes — Catherine has trained leaders and teams across seven continents, equipping them with the tools to communicate with clarity, confidence, and compassion.

Through *Leading Ladies Lunches* and global retreats, she empowers women to embrace their unique journey, build their leadership skills, share their stories, and strengthen their legacy.

In *EmpowHer*, Catherine combines wisdom, warmth, and experience to remind us that empowered women empower the world — and that leadership begins not with a title, but with the courage to make a difference. She shares her belief that every woman holds the power to influence, uplift, and ignite change — one conversation, one connection, one courageous act at a time.

🌐 www.CatherineMolloy.com.au

 catherinemolloy

Acknowledgments

To every woman who has poured her truth into these pages — thank you. Your courage, wisdom, and lived experience are a gift to the world, and it is an honour to stand beside you as we write history together.

To dear Andrea and Putting Words, we can't thank you enough, for your commitment and making the process so easy. To your editors, designers, and support team—your dedication has shaped these stories into a lasting legacy.

To the families, friends, and communities who encouraged each of us to share our voices — your support matters. You make it possible for women's stories to rise, to be heard, and to inspire change.

And finally, to the women who will read this book, may these stories remind you of your power. May they challenge you, uplift you, and invite you to lead with purpose and heart.

Together, we rise.

With gratitude,

Catherine Molloy

LEADING LADIES LUNCHES
LEARN. LEVERAGE. LEAD

Leadingladieslunches.com

Join free monthly webinars

Join the membership only US$88 for a whole year
- receive the monthly toolkit
- monthly leadership conversations world wide
- downloadable book the conscious leader
- plus 6 leadership workshops

Buy 1 membership give 1 to help some of our poorest women in the world helping others.

Join yearly leadership retreats and writers' retreats.